BURMESE
SELF TAUGHT

Marlborough's Self-Taught Series-No. 25.

BURMESE SELF TAUGHT

(IN BURMESE AND ROMAN CHARACTERS) WITH

PHONETIC PRONUNCIATION.

(THIMM'S SYSTEM.)

BY

R. F. St. A. St. JOHN, HON. M.A. (Oxon.),

Author of "A Burmese Reader."

(Sometime Lecturer on Burmese, Universities of Oxford and Cambridge).

GYAN

Published by

GYAN

Gyan Publishing House
5, Ansari Road
Daryaganj, New Delhi-110002
Phone: 011-47034999, 9811692060
E-mail: books@gyanbooks.com

Distribution Network
gyanbooks.com
India, USA, Canada, UK, Australia, France

ISBN : 978-81-212-4257-8 (PB)
First Published, 1911

2nd Impression 2020

Printed at: Gyan Press, Delhi.

Burmese Self Taught
Author: St. John

MARLBOROUGH'S SELF-TAUGHT SERIES—No. 25.

Burmese Self-Taught

(IN BURMESE AND ROMAN CHARACTERS)

WITH

PHONETIC PRONUNCIATION.

(THIMM'S SYSTEM.)

BY

R. F. St. A. St. JOHN, Hon. M.A. (Oxon.),

Author of "A Burmese Reader."

(Sometime Lecturer on Burmese, Universities of Oxford and Cambridge).

E. MARLBOROUGH & CO., 51, OLD BAILEY, LONDON, E.C.

1911.

PREFACE.

THIS manual of Burmese is designed to serve the double purpose of a text-book for students, missionaries, officers, civil servants, etc., and a handbook for tourists, travellers, and other temporary visitors to Burma.

For those whom the pleasures of travel or the calls of trade and commerce bring into touch with native Burmans, a very extensive and comprehensive vocabulary of necessary and useful words is supplied—nouns, verbs, adjectives and other parts of speech—together with corresponding collections of colloquial phrases and sentences of an equally practical and useful character. These are all classified under subject-titles for easy reference, and the phonetic pronunciation of the Burmese words is added in a third column, in accordance with Marlborough's popular phonetic system. Thus, a tourist, traveller, or trader, with no previous knowledge of the language, can readily make himself understood amongst the Burmese by means of this volume.

On the other hand, the opening section, pp. 9-28, and the outline of Grammar, pp. 107-126, will meet the additional needs of students and all who desire a closer acquaintance with the language.

The method of presenting the English words and sentences, the Burmese equivalents, and the phonetic pronunciation of the Burmese words, side by side, will not only enable the book to be used by stray visitors to the country, but assist those who intend to make Burma their sphere of work and enable them to learn the language in the only way in which it ought to be learned.

The underlying idea of the system of phonetics employed is that each sound in the Burmese language is represented as far as possible by a separate phonetic sign, and consequently each sign (letter or combination of letters) must always be pronounced in the same manner.

A few of these signs are necessarily of a more or less arbitrary character, and the introduction of the tone or accent marks adds a certain amount of strangeness to them. The student will do well therefore to read the scheme of phonetics with great care, this being the key to the correct pronunciation of the Burmese, as represented in the third column of the Vocabularies and Conversations.

Burmese, or, as the people of Burma call it, *Myanmā hbātha* (the language of the Myanmā), is the speech of a considerable and powerful tribe, closely connected with the Tibetans, which, prior to A.D. 1000, over-ran the valley of the Irrawaddy River, and adopted Buddhism and the alphabet of its sacred books—which were written in Pali, an alphabet founded on the ancient characters of India. [The Burmese call themselves Bă*h*mā*h*, and this word has nothing to do, as some suppose, with Brahman, which word exists in Burmese as Byăhmă*h*nā*h*. It is a natural corruption of Mră*h*nmā*h*. The original name of the tribe was Mră*h*n, which in Pali became Mră*h*nmo*h*, plural Mră*h*nmā*h*—pronounced quickly Bă*h*mā*h*.]

The language is monosyllabic and agglutinative, having neither conjugation nor declension; so that, in almost every instance, its composite words can be taken to pieces and the power of each part clearly shown. At the outset it would seem that it consisted of monosyllabic roots which denoted either a substance or an act, such as dog, iron, fire, stone, do, run, stop. From the verbal root came a verbal noun, which was formed by prefixing "a" (ă*h*) to the verb root; simple verb roots were used to denote case, mood, tense, and also other parts of speech.

As Burmese has adopted words from the Pali language, all the letters of the alphabet are in use, but for pure Burmese words those classified as cerebral, and one or two others, are not used.

The Author is indebted to Mr. Po Han, B.A., a native of Burma, for valuable assistance in reading the proofs of the work, and has himself spared no pains to make it thoroughly accurate and reliable, and capable of proving a practical guide to the spoken tongue, and a valuable introduction to the study and mastery cf the language.

London, 1911.

CONTENTS.

Outlines of Burmese Grammar:— PAGE

Conversational Phrases and Sentences:—

Money, Weights, and Measures:—

"A GLIMPSE OF BURMA"

[*Extracted from an article by Dr. Francis E. Clark in the* CHRISTIAN WORLD *of February 3rd, 1910, by kind permission of the Editor.*]

IT is not too much to say that Burma contains more of interest than any equal section of the Indian Empire.

Many people think of Burma as a part of India, and the Burmese as Indians, but they are no more Indians than the Chinese are Americans. To be sure, Burma is a province of the Indian Empire, though it ought to be as much a separate dominion as Australia or Canada.

It is a three days' journey on a fast steamer from Calcutta to Rangoon; and when one reaches the latter city he finds people of a totally different race, different language, different customs, different complexion, different costumes and different religion.

He finds that he has exchanged the sun-parched fields of India, where famine always stalks behind the labourer, for the well-watered meadows of the Irrawaddy, where in December the luxuriant fields of rice wave their heavy tasselled heads, and where all the year round and the century through famine is unknown.

Instead of the straight-featured, thin-limbed, agile Aryans whom he left in Calcutta, the traveller finds in Rangoon, three or four days later, round-faced, jolly, plump Mongolians, with slant eyes and yellow skins, and the merriest of black, twinkling eyes.

Instead of the three-and-thirty million gods, whom he saw worshipped in Benares, he finds no god in Rangoon, but only the placid, unwinking, half-smiling image of Gautama Buddha, who, five hundred years before Christ, attained to Nirvana, and whose image is to-day worshipped by one-third of the human race.

In India, one finds temples carved with all sorts of curious and often hideous figures of everything that is in heaven above and the earth beneath and the waters under the earth. In Burma, graceful, slender pagodas, often encrusted thickly with gold leaf, and rising from fifty to three hundred feet in the air, are seen; and everywhere, in every stately pagoda and every little jewelled shrine, the same image, calm, unseeing, immovable to earthly joys or sorrows, Gautama, as he attained the long-sought Nirvana.

Next to Bombay and Calcutta, Rangoon is the busiest port in the Indian Empire. Here are great godowns, or wholesale storehouses, filled with the choicest wares and products of the East, large department stores, . . . public buildings, post-office, custom-house, &c., that would do credit to any city in the world. Here, too, is a beautiful public park, charming lakes, an extensive Zoo, all in the heart of the city.

The spot to which all travellers' paths converge in Rangoon is the Shwe Dagon Pagoda, the most sacred spot in all the Buddhist world. Up a long flight of stone steps we walk, on either side of which are chattering vendors of curious wares—silks and lace and gongs of brass, huge cheroots, eight or ten inches long, and as large round as your two thumbs, which contain tobacco enough for a family smoke, oranges, mangoes, jack-fruit and papaws, jade ornaments and tinsel jewels—indeed, almost anything that a Burman would want to eat or wear or bedeck himself with.

At the top of the steps a gorgeous, glittering sight indeed strikes the eye, for there rises a great and graceful column of gold, a hundred and fifty feet above the vast platform on which it is built, and which itself rises one hundred and seventy feet from the ground. The pagoda is very wide at the base, and tapers gradually to a ball-shaped top, on which is a crown of solid gold and jewels alone worth a round half-million dollars.

All around are little pagodas, or shrines, clustering close to the base of the parent, and each vying with all the others to show itself the richest and most bejewelled.

In the great pagoda is a huge Buddha, so covered with gold and gems that the covetous public is kept away from it by strong iron bars, while all the lesser shrines have other images of the placid saint, and some of them many, but all with exactly the same expression of ineffable content.

A multitude of other sights, odd, beautiful, bizarre, but all interesting, attract the traveller,

On the road to Mandalay,

which lies some twenty hours' journey up the Irrawaddy. They are well worth the notice of anyone who can wander from the beaten tracks of travel long enough to enjoy them.

BURMESE SELF-TAUGHT.

THE ALPHABET AND PRONUNCIATION.

The alphabet used by the Burmese is of Indian origin and came to them through Buddhist monks. It is commonly called *Pali.* It consists of thirty-two consonants and eight primary vowels. There are three diphthongs, and the vowel sounds are further modified by final consonants.

Only twenty-five of the consonants are used in Burmese words, but the whole are put into requisition for words borrowed from the Pali.

As the Burmese (except the Arracanese branch) cannot pronounce the letter r they substitute y for it, so that y is represented by both r and y, and they are often interchanged in writing, though it has been agreed that certain words shall be written with r and certain with y.

What is generally known as romanization,—i.e. the transliteration into Roman characters,—when applied to Burmese does not answer, so there are many systems of representing the sounds of the language in use, viz. those of Judson, Latter, Chase, Tawseinko, and the Government, or Hunterian.

The plan adopted in this work, however, is to give the words in the native character throughout, and instead of attempting to romanize the characters, to add the phonetic pronunciation of the words in accordance with the following scheme, which is based upon Marlborough's system of phonetics.

CONSONANTS.[1]

Burmese Characters.	Romanized form.	Pronunciation.	Phonetics used.
က	k	When initial like *k* in *kite*; when final sometimes like *t* and sometimes *k*: after a word ending with a vowel or nasal as *g* in *gate*[2] . . .	k, t, g
ခ	hk	When initial before y like *ch* in *chair*; when following a vowel or nasal like *j* in *joint*	hk ch, j
ဂ	g	Like *g* in *gate*; never final; with y like *j* in *joint* or *jig*	g, j
ဃ	hg	Not used in Burmese words; like *g* in *gate*; when final mute	g
င	gn	As in *agnostic* with the *a* swallowed . .	gn
		When final like *n* or *ng*	n, ng
စ	ts	When final like *t* in *pit*; changes to *z*	ts, z, t
ဆ	hs	Like *s* in *see*; after vowel or nasal changes to *z*	s, z
ဇ	z	As *z* in *zebra*; when final like *t* in *pit*	z, t
ဈ	z		
ည	ny	Like *ny* in *Bunyan*	ny
		When final sometimes like *n* in *pin*; sometimes a simple ĕĕ sound as in *bee*, and sometimes as *eh*	n ĕĕ eh
တ	t	When initial as *t* in *ten* or (when following) *d* in *den*	t, d
		When final something between t and p and k final	t, p, k
ထ	ht	When initial *ht* or (when following a vowel or nasal) *d* in *den*	ht, d
ဒ	d	When initial as *d* in *den*	d
		When final, between *t* and *k*	t, k
ဓ	hd	As *d* in *den*	d

[1] The Cerebrals are omitted as they are not used for Burmese and correspond with the Dentals.

[2] See para. (*f*), p. 22.

Burmese Characters.	Romanized form.	Pronunciation.	Phonetics used.
န	n	When initial as *n* in *not*; when final as *n* in *hen* and sometimes slightly like *ng* after o	n, ng
ပ	p	When initial as *p* in *pen*; changes[1] to *b* in *bed*	p, b
		When final same as for တ	t, p, k
ဖ	hp	When initial *hp*; when following[1] a vowel or nasal *b*	hp, b
ဗ	b	Initial like *b* in *bed*	b
ဘ	hb	Initial sometimes as *b* in *bed*; . .	b
		sometimes as *hp*	hb, hp
မ	m	When initial like *m*; when final like *n* or *ng*	m, n, ng
ယ	y	When initial as *y* in *yet*, when final *eh*.	y, eh
ရ	r, y	When initial *y*, when final as *eh* . .	y, eh
လ	l	Initial as *l* in *let*; when final mute . . .	l
ဝ	w	Initial as in English; medial as *ŏŏ*; final mute	w, ŏŏ
ဠ	l	When used in Pali derivatives like English *l*.	l
သ	th	Initial as *th* in *thin*	th
		Changes after final vowel or nasal to *th* in *that*; as final or medial, *t*	t
ဟ	h	As initial *h* in English: may be placed before all consonants which have not an aspirate form; if final mute	h
ံ	n	Used instead of န *n* or မ *m*;	n
		with ေါ *aw* becomes like *k*	k

Note.—It is impossible to give examples of the way in which ts, ht, hd, hp, and hb are to be pronounced as initials, but the student must endeavour to sound the letters together in their written order, for ts, ht, and hp. Hd and hb are merely a stronger d and b.

[1] The words 'following' and 'changes' refer to rule (*f*.), p. 22.

VOWELS AND DIPHTHONGS.

Burmese.	Romanized.	Pronunciation.	Phonetics.
အ	a	Like *a* in *father* but short . .	ăh
အာ	â	„ *a* in *father*	âh
ဣ။အိ	i	„ *i* in *machinery* but shorter	ĕē
ဤ။အီ	ee	„ *ee* in *feet*	ee
ဥ။အု	u	„ *oo* in *foot*	ŏŏ
ဦ။အူ	ū	„ *oo* in *boot*	oo
ဧ။အေ	é	„ *a* in *holiday*	ay
အဲ	è	„ the first *e* in *there* . .	eh
အော	aw	*aw* as in *paw*	aw
အော်	āw	Longer and drawn out . . .	āw
အို	o	Like *o* in *go*	oh
အိုး	ô	Deeper and long drawn out .	ôh:
အို့	ŏ	Sharp and short	ŏẖ
ွ[1]	w	Like *oo* in *foot*, or Welsh w .	ŏŏ
ွိ[1]	w	Like *oo* in *spoon*.	oo

VOWELS AND DIPHTHONGS WITH FINALS.

အက် ăh followed by k is like *e* in *let*.

အစ် ăh followed by ts is like *i* in *pit*.

အင် ăh followed by gn is like *i* and *e* in *tin* and *ten*.

အည် ăh followed by ny is like *ee* or *in* or *eh*.

အပ်, အတ်, အန်, အမ်, အံ ; ăh followed by any of these retains its sound as *a* in *can't* (ăh).

အိပ်, အိတ်, အိန်, အိမ် ; i (ee) followed by these consonants is like *ai* in *bait* (ay).

[1] အ cannot be used with ွ.

အုပ်, အုတ်, အုန်, အုမ်, အုံ ; ŭ (ŏŏ) followed by these, like *o* in *bone* (o*h*).

အယ် è as first *e* in *there* (eh).

အောက်, အောင် ; éā followed by k or gn, as *ow* in *how* (ow).

အိုက်, အိုင် ; iu followed by k or gn, like *i* in *pine* (i)

The alphabet is classified as below. Every consonant contains an inherent ă (ă*h*) which has to be pronounced with it until killed by the mark ် (thă*h*t = strike *or* kill) placed over it, or until it is modified by a final.[1]

Thus က k must be kă*h* until it is killed—က်, and it then has the sound of the final *t* in *let*.

Gutturals	က kă*h*	ခ hkă*h*	ဂ gă*h*	ဃ hgă*h*	င ngă*h*
Palatals	စ tsă*h*	ဆ hsă*h*	ဇ dză*h*	ဈ hdzăh	ည nyă*h*
Cerebrals	ဋ ţă*h*	ဌ htă*h*	ဍ dă*h*	ဎ hdă*h*	ဏ nă*h*
Dentals	တ tă*h*	ထ htă*h*	ဒ dă*h*	ဓ hdă*h*	န nă*h*
Labials	ပ pă*h*	ဖ hpă*h*	ဗ bă*h*	ဘ hbă*h*	မ mă*h*
Liquids	ယ yă*h*	ရ ră*h*	လ lă*h*	ဝ wă*h*	ဠ llă*h*
Sibilant	သ thă*h*				
Aspirate	ဟ hă*h*				

The ဆ hts is pronounced as s.

The ဘ hb is often used instead of ဖ hp.

ဈ hdz is exactly the same as ဇ dz and only used in one common Burmese word.

The cerebrals with ဃ hg and ဠ ll are only used in words derived from Pali.

The cerebrals are essentially Indian, Pali, or Sanskrit. The Burmese cannot differentiate them from the dentals,

[1] See under 'Final Consonants', p. 18.

and so pronounce them when used, and also the liquid ll, in the same way as the dentals.

The ဂ g and ဃ hg are pronounced the same.

င is pronounced like ung-*ăh*, low down in the throat, and when aspirated nothing can describe it.

ရ r is not pronounceable by a Burman (except the Arracanese branch) but is pronounced as ယ y and the two letters are interchangeable.

Every letter which has not an aspirate form can be aspirated by the addition of the sign for ဟ hă*h* ှ written under it; thus န nă*h* when aspirated is written နှ hnă*h*, လ lá*h* လှ hlá*h*. When ယ yă*h* and ရ yă*h* are aspirated they become ယှ ရှ shă*h*.

သ has two sounds as *th* in *thin* and *th* in *that*.

Neither ဘ nor ဟ can take the aspirate.

Certain consonants are capable of combination with the others so as to be pronounced as one. This is done by means of a secondary form as shown in the following table:—

Consonants	ယ	ရ	ဝ	ဟ	ယ + ဝ	ရ + ဝ	ယ + ဟ
Second forms	ျ	ြ	ွ	ှ	ျွ	ြွ	ျှ

Consonants (*cont.*)	ရ + ဟ	ဝ + ဟ	ရ + ဟ + ွ	
Second forms (*cont.*)	ြှ	ွှ	ြွှ	

The force of these combinations is best shown with the consonant မ mă*h*, which alone can take the whole.

မ mă*h* မျ myă*h* မြ myă*h* မွ mwă*h* မှ hmă*h*

မျွ myŏŏă*h* မြွ myŏŏă*h* (like mew-ă*h*)

မျှ hmyă*h* မြှ hmyă*h* မွှ hmwă*h* မြွှ hmyŏŏă*h*

ဂြ gnyă*h* and ည nyă*h* have the same sound and are interchangeable.

In addition to the final consonants there is also the sign ံ, called သေးသေးတင် thay:*th*ay:tin, which is written above a consonant and has the power of final n, as ကံ = ကန် kă*h*n. When used with the diphthong အော aw it has the power of final k, as အောံ = အောက် owk.

VOWELS AND DIPHTHONGS.

There are eight written vowels and three diphthongs.

Short vowels : အ ă*h* ဣ ĕĕ ဥ ŏŏ

Long vowels : အာ ā*h* ဤ ee ဦ oo ဧ ay အဲ e*h*

Diphthongs : ဩ or အော aw ဪ or အော် āw အို o*h*

To unite these vowels and diphthongs to the various consonants certain secondary forms are required which are usually called symbols.

အ ă*h* being inherent in every consonant has none.

အာ ā*h*	ာ or ါ	as ကာ kā*h* ဝါ wā*h*
ဣ ĕĕ	ိ	as ကိ kĕĕ
ဤ ee	ီ	as ကီ kee
ဥ ŏŏ	ု	as ကု kŏŏ
ဦ oo	ူ	as ကူ koo
ဧ ay	ေ	as ကေ kay
အဲ eh	ဲ	as ကဲ keh
ဩ aw	ေ – ာ	as ကော kaw
ဪ āw . . .	ေ – ာ်	as ကော် kāw
အို o*h*	ို	as ကို ko*h*

The forms ဣ ဤ ဥ ဦ are as a rule used only for Pali words, the vowel အ with secondary forms being used instead, thus:—အိ ĕĕ အီ ee အု ŏŏ အူ oo.

The vowels can thus be united to all the consonants and

double consonants in the same way, and, it will be observed, replace the inherent အ ă*h*.

The two forms ာ and ါ for long ā*h* are to prevent confusion. If ာ were used with ဝ wă*h* it would become ထ tă*h*, so we must use ဝါ wā*h*.

NOTES ON COMBINED CONSONANTS AND VOWELS.

The y sound when joined to another consonant must be sounded as much as possible with it; ကြ ကျ are kyă*h*, not ky-ȧ*h*. ခြ hkyă*h* is chă*h*. ဂြ jă*h*.

Some combinations are very easy, as—

ရှ	ရှာ	ရှိ	ရှီ	ရှု	ရှူ	ရှေ	
လျှ	လျှာ	လျှိ	လျှီ	လျှု	လျှူ	လျှေ	&c.
shă*h*	shā*h*	shĕĕ	shee	shŏŏ	shoo	shay	

The consonant ဝ wă*h* in combination is sometimes a consonant and sometimes a vowel.

မွ is hmwă*h*, but မြွ is myŏŏă*h* (mew-ă*h*).

NOTE.—*Ky*, *gy*, &c., are sounded in all shades from *k* and *g* to *ch* in *church* and *j* in *judge*.

Some examples of Consonants combined with Vowel symbols:—

VOWELS.

ခ hkă*h*	ခါ hkā*h*	ခိ hkëë	ခီ hkee	ခု hkŏŏ	ခူ hkoo	ခေ hkay	ခဲ hkeh
ည nyă*h*	ညာ nyā*h*	ညိ nyëë	ညီ nyee	ညု nyŏŏ	ညူ nyoo	ညေ nyay	ညဲ nye
ပ pă*h*	ပါ pā*h*	ပိ pëë	ပီ pee	ပု pŏŏ	ပူ poo	ပေ pay	ပဲ peh
ယ yă*h*	ယာ yā*h*	ယိ yëë	ယီ yee	ယု yŏŏ	ယူ yoo	ယေ yay	ယဲ yeh
ဝ wă*h*	ဝါ wāh	ဝိ wëë	ဝီ wee	ဝု wŏŏ	ဝူ woo	ဝေ way	ဝဲ weh

DIPHTHONGS.

ဂေါ gaw	ဂေါ် gāw	ဂို go*h*	ငေါ gnaw	ငေါ် gnāw	ငို gno*h*
စော tsaw	စော် tsāw	စို tso*h*	ဒေါ daw	ဒေါ် dāw	ဒို do*h*
တော taw	တော် tāw	တို to*h*	ထော thaw	ထော် thāw	ထို tho*h*
ယော yaw	ယော် yāw	ယို yo*h*	ဖေါ hpaw	ဖေါ် hpāw	ဖို hpo*h*

COMBINED CONSONANTS WITH VOWELS.

ကျ kyă*h* ကျာ kyā*h* ကျိ kyĕĕ ကျီ kyee ကျု kyŏŏ ကျူ kyoo ကျေ kyay ကျဲ kyeh ကြ kyă*h* ကြာ kyā*h* ကြိ kyĕĕ ကြီ kyee ကြု kyŏŏ ကြူ kyoo ကြေ kyay ကြဲ kyeh.[1]

ချ chă*h* ချာ chā*h* ချိ chĕĕ ချီ chee ချု chŏŏ ချူ choo ချေ chay ချဲ cheh ခြ chă*h* ခြာ chā*h* ခြိ chĕĕ ခြီ chee ခြု chŏŏ ခြူ choo ခြေ chay ခြဲ cheh.

ပွ pwă*h* ပွါ pwā*h* ပွိ pwĕĕ ပွီ pwee ပွေ pway ပွဲ pweh.

လွ lwă*h* လွာ lwā*h* လွိ lwĕĕ လွီ lwee လွေ lway လွဲ lweh.

(In this last combination the ွ almost amounts to ŏŏ.)

ငှ hgnă*h* ငှာ hgnā*h* ညှိ hnyĕĕ ညှု hnyŏŏ ညှော hnyaw ညှို hnyo*h* လှ hlă*h* လှာ hlā*h* လှိ hlĕĕ လှီ hlee လှု hlŏŏ လှူ hloo လှေ hlay လှဲ hleh.

ကျွ / ကြွ } kyŏŏ-ă*h* ကျွာ / ကြွာ } kyŏŏ-ā*h* ကျွိ / ကြွိ } kyŏŏ-ĕĕ ကျွေ / ကြွေ } kyŏŏ-ay ကျွဲ / ကြွဲ } kyŏŏ-eh.

နွှာ hnwā*h* မွှာ hmwā*h* လွှာ hlwā*h* လွှေ hlway လွှဲ hlweh.

[1] Hky, gy with the vowels are sounded in many shades from *k* and *g* to *ch* in church and *j* in judge, and no rule can be given. With the vowel e (ay) the sound of the vowel varies, as ခြေ chay is often pronounced as if it were chĕĕ and ကျေး kyay: as kyee:.

လျှ is pronounced in two ways—hlyă*h* and shă*h*; so we get

လျှာ } shā*h* ရှာ — လျှော } shaw ရှော — လျှို } sho*h* ရှို

Occasionally one finds the combination of ြ yă*h* ွ wă*h* and ှ hă*h*, but it is pronounced with ြ yă*h* omitted, so that မြွှ hmyŏŏ-ăh = မွှ hmwă*h*.

FINAL CONSONANTS.

Other vowel sounds are obtained by means of a final consonant.

A consonant is made final by placing over it the mark ်, which is called သတ် *that* (thá*h*t, kill). It is so called because it kills the inherent အ ă*h*.

Thus, ကတ is *kata*, but ကတ် is *kat*.
ကက is *kaka*, but ကက် is *ket*.
လော is *law*, but လောက် is *lowk*.
တို is *to*, but တိုင် is *taing* or ting.
တစ is *tatsa*, but တစ် is *tit*.

The same thing occurs when two consonants come together in a foreign word of more than one syllable, and one consonant is written under the other; thus,

ဓမ္မ hdammă*h*, *law* (pronounced dă*h*mă*h*).
ပုဏ္ဏား puññā*h*:, *a Brahmin* (pronounced po*h*nnā*h*:).
ဘဏ္ဍာ hbañḍā*h*, *property* (pronounced hpădā*h*).

This is also allowable in a few Burmese words which have become stereotyped; as,

မိန္မ for မိန်းမ mayn:mă*h*, *a woman*.

This word also shows another rule as to the interchange

of final မ măh and န năh. The final မ် is considered heavier than န် and is equal to န်း. When two l's come together thus လ္လ, as in လုလ္လ, the first l changes to *n*, so instead of lŏŏllă*h* we get lo*h*nlă*h*.

Though several consonants are written as final, there are really only four final sounds, viz. k, t, ng, n.

Final consonants are very indistinct, and not only is the inherent အ ă*h* killed, but the consonant itself is almost done away with, and it is almost impossible to say whether the sharp, abrupt sound is k, t, or p.

The effect of final consonants on the preceding vowels is shown in the following table:—

Final consonant.	Combined with vowels and w.						Power.
	ă*h* အ	ĕĕ ဣ	ŏŏ ဥ	o*h* အို	aw ဪ	w ဝ	
က် k	et			ik	owk		
င် ng	in			ing	owng		
စ် ts	it						
ည် ñ	eh						This final has three sounds, ĕĕ, eh, in.
တ် t or ပ် p	ă*h*t	ayk	o*h*k			ŏŏt	As in root.
န် n or မ် m ံ	ă*h*n	ayn	o*h*n			ŏŏn	The မ် makes the vowel heavier.
ယ် y	eh						

These sounds should be practised with all the consonants; thus,

ကက် ket ကင် kin ကစ် kit ကည် kĕĕ.

ကတ် kă*h*t ကပ် kă*h*t ကန် kă*h*n ကမ် kă*h*n.

ကံ kă*h*n ကန်း kā*h*n: ကယ် keh.

ကိုက် kik ကိုင် king.

ကိတ် kayt ကိန် kayn.

ကုပ် or ကုတ် ko*h*k ကုန် or ကုံ ko*h*n ကုမ် ko*h*n.

ကွတ် or ကွပ် kŏŏt ကွန် or ကွံ kŏŏn ကွမ် koon.

No matter what consonant or double consonant begins the word, the vowels always remain as above; thus,

ဆင် sin ဝင် win ချင် chin တွင် twin ရှင် shin.

စစ် tsit ညစ် nyit ခြစ် chit လှစ် hlit မျှစ် hmyit.

In the following combination some words seem to end with t and some with k:—

ဆိတ် sayt တိတ် tayt ချိတ် chayt မိတ် mayt.

အိပ် ayk ရိတ် yayk လိပ် layk သိတ် thayk.

လုပ် lo*h*k ဆုတ် so*h*k ချုပ် cho*h*k ငုတ် hgno*h*k.

ဝ wă*h* is w with all consonants without a final, except ည nyă*h* ယ yă*h* ရ yă*h*, when it takes the vowel sound, as ညွ nyooă*h* ရွ yooă*h*.

မျှ hmyă*h* မျှီ hmyĕĕ မျှု hmyŏŏ မျှေ hmyay.

ကွ kwă*h* ဂွီ gwĕĕ ငွေ gnway ကျွဲ kyŏŏ-eh.

In certain words taken from the Pali we find a final quiescent consonant—

ကိုယ် ko*h* မိုဃ် mo*h* မိုရ် mo*h*.

ဗိုလ် bo*h* ဖိုလ် hpo*h* ဂြိုဟ် jo*h*.

The double သ thă*h* is written ဿ and pronounced tth, as ကဿပ kă*h*t-thă*h*-pă*h* or kth as in ဥဿုံ o*h*k-tho*h*n. The Pali pronunciation of these would be kassapa and ussun.

TONES OR ACCENTS.

There are three tones :—

(*a*) The ordinary (unmarked), as မြင် myin, *to see.*

(*b*) The abrupt, (a small circle written under the word), as မြင့် myin̥, *lofty, tall.*

(*c*) The prolonged heavy tone, (two small circles following the word), as မြင်း myin: (or myeen:), *a horse.*

The light accent may be used with final ေအ ay, အဲ eh, ေအာ aw, အို ŏh, or a mute nasal consonant, as ကန့် kăhn̥.

The heavy accent may follow အာ āh, အီ ee, အူ oo, ေအ ay, အဲ eh, အို oh, and the mute nasal consonants, as တင်း tin, တုန်း tôhn:.

By means of these accents, or cadences, three distinct meanings can be given ; as,

myin, *to see* ; myin̥, *tall, high* ; myinး, *a* horse.

PHONETIC CHANGES.

(*a*) When a final consonant is followed by a nasal it is assimilated ; as,

အိပ်မက် ayk-met, *to dream*, becomes ayn-met.

ေအာက်မေ့ owk-may̥, *to long for*, becomes owng-may̥.

နိုင်နာ nit-nāh, *to be aggrieved*, becomes nin-nāh.

(*b*) Sometimes the vowels ŏŏ and oo are elided ; as,

ပုရပိုက် pŏŏ-yăh-bik, *a note-book*, becomes păh-yăh-bik.

(*c*) The letters ဘ băh, ပ păh, and မ măh are interchangeable ; as,

ထဘီ htăh-bee, *a petticoat*, becomes htah-mee.

ဓါးပြ hdāhး-pyah, *a bandit*, becomes hdąhး-myăh.

(*d*) Words beginning with ŏŏ and oo take the initial consonant of the following syllable; as,

ဥမှင် ŏŏ-hmin, *a cave*, becomes o*h*n(m)-hmin.
ဦးနှောက် oo-hnowk, *brains*, becomes ô*h*n:-hnowk.
ဦးခေါင် oo-hkowng, *head*, becomes o*h*k-hkowng.

(*e*) The final nasal of the first syllable is sometimes dropped; as,

ဆံပင် sáhn-pin, *hair of the head*, becomes să*h*-bin.
တံခါး tă*h*n-hkā*h*:, *a door*, becomes tă*h*-gā*h*:.
ပန်းပဲး pă*h*n:-peh:, *a blacksmith*, becomes pă*h*-beh:.[1]

(*f*) When a word ending with a vowel or nasal precedes another so as to form as it were a polysyllable, and the initial consonant of the following word is one of those in columns 1 and 2 on p. 13, it must as a rule be changed to the corresponding consonant in col. 3 or col. 4; thus,

သင်ခြင် sin-chin, *to consider*, becomes sin-jin.
ဖြစ်ခဲ့စွာတကား hpyit-hkeh-tsŏŏā*h* tá*h*-kā*h*: becomes hpyit-hkeh-zŏŏā*h* tá*h*-gā*h*:.

NUMERALS.[2]

1	2	3	4	5	6	7	8	9	0
၁	၂	၃	၄	၅	၆	၇	၈	၉	၀

These figures are used exactly like the English figures.

WRITING.

Burmese is written from left to right, but there is little use for punctuation as the sentences punctuate themselves. A full stop may be represented by ။ and to divide paragraphs ။ ။ is used.

[1] The heavy accent on the first word is often dropped in compounds.
[2] See p. 78, and p. 114.

ABBREVIATIONS IN COMMON USE.

၏ for ဧည့် ee at the end of a sentence, or *of.*
ေင့် „ ကြောင့် jowng, *because.*
ေင်း „ ကောင်း kowng:, *good.*
၌ „ နှိုက် hnik, *in, at.*
၍ „ ရွေ့ yŏŏgy, *and.*
၎င် „ လည်းကောင်း lee: gowng:, *both — and; the aforesaid.*
လုင် „ လုလင် lŏŏlin, *a bachelor.*
ႆ „ င် written over as in သင်္ဘော for သင်းဘော thim: baw, *a ship.*

PRELIMINARY NOTES.

The foregoing pages, 9–22, should be carefully read and the phonetic equivalents of the Burmese characters noted. Practice in copying the characters themselves will soon enable the student to read and write the words and phrases in the following lists, which he is also recommended to learn by heart, repeating them aloud with the aid of the phonetic spelling in the third column.

PRONUNCIATION.—It will be noticed that the values of the vowels in the Pronunciation column are not always the same. This is caused by euphony, as, for instance, in '*ă*h-nā*h*-zô*h*:'. This is the correct transliteration, but the pronunciation is '*ă*h-nă*h*-zô*h*:'.

TONES OR ACCENTS.—For the proper appreciation and correct use of these, the student is recommended to avail himself of every opportunity of getting native tutorial assistance. They are usually indicated in the phonetic pronunciation, which of course would be imperfect without them. In the Burmese text they are always shown, but some do not appear in the 'pronunciation' column. The reason is that when words are run together as compounds, the heavy tone is often rejected and the ictus thrown on to the last word.

For instance, တရား tă*h*-yā*h*: (*law*), when turned into 'civil law' by the addition of မ mă*h*, becomes တရားမ tă*h*-yă*h*-măh'.

The heavy accent : is supposed to be inherent in the vowel အဲ eh:, unless superseded by the light accent, and is not, as a rule, written. Therefore လဲ leh is properly leh:. We find it written, however, with ကဲး၊ ဝဲး and one or two other words.

THE USE OF THE HYPHEN.—It has been the custom in transliterating Burmese words to put a hyphen indiscriminately between every syllable and the next; thus—

*Th*ee-ă*h*-yă*h*t-hmā*h*-gnā*h*-ă*h*-yin-tă*h*-hkā*h*-hmyă*h*-mă*h*-yowk-tsă*h*-hpoo:-boo:.

This seems a very senseless method as it shows nothing. In this work, only those syllables which are really connected together in a composite manner are so joined, and the above sentence would be written as under—

*Th*ee	ă*h*-yă*h*t-hmā*h*	gnā*h*	ă*h*-yin	tă*h*-hkā*h*-hmyă*h*	mă*h*
This	*place - in*	*I*	*before*	*one-time-even* (*once*)	*not*

yowk-tsă*h* - hpoo:-boo:.
arrive (assertive affixes).

It was found, however, that this plan could not always be strictly adhered to, as the syllables of some composite words required proper division, for example, it would not have been possible to write the word ă*h*-yă*h*t as ă*h*yă*h*t.

The hyphen has therefore been used in two ways—(*a*) to connect words which form polysyllabic expressions; (*b*) to separate syllables that might be mispronounced if written as one word.

HINTS ON ADDRESSING A BURMAN.—Do not raise the voice or shout, and speak slowly and distinctly.

Be careful not to drop the aspirate. There is a great difference between p and hp, t and ht, but no practical difference between b and hb, d and hd.

Be very careful to differentiate the sounds ay and eh; for instance, အမေ ă*h*-may is *mother* and အမဲး ă*h*-meh: is *game*; လှေ hlay *canoe* and လှည်း hleh: *a cart*. In the latter case there can be no mistake if the proper numeral auxiliary is used; thus လှေတစင်း hlay-tă*h*-zin: and လှည်းတစီး hleh:-tă*h*-zee:.

Remember the rule as to change in consonants (p. 22, *f*).

VOCABULARIES.

The World and its Elements. ပထဝီမြေကြီးနှင့်ဓါတ်များ။

English	Burmese.	Pronunciation.
air	လေ	lay
cloud	မိုဃ်းတိမ်	mô*h*:-dayn
cold	ေခြင်း။ အအေး	ay-jin:, ă*h*-ay:
comet	ကြယ်တံခွန်	kyeh-tă*h*-gŏŏn
darkness	မိုက်ခြင်း	mik-chin:
dew *or* fog	နှင်း။ ဆီးနှင်း	hnin:, see:-hnin:
dust	အမှုန်။ ဖုတ်	á*h*-hmo*h*n, hpo*h*k
earth	မြေ။ မြေကြီး	myay, myay-jee:
earthquake	မြေကြီးလှုပ်ခြင်း	myay-jee: hlo*h*k-chin:
east	အရှေ့	ă*h*-shay
eclipse (of sun)	နေကြတ်ခြင်း	nay-kyă*h*t-chin:
— (of moon)	လကြတ်ခြင်း	lă*h*-kyă*h*t-chin:
fire	မီး	mee:
flame	မီးလျှံ	mee:-shă*h*n
frost	ဆီးခဲ	see:-geh
hail	မိုဃ်းသီး	mô*h*:-*th*ee:
heat	အပူ	ă*h*-poo
light	အလင်း	ă*h*-lin:
lightning	လျှပ်စစ်	shă*h*t-tsit
moon; new, full	လ။ လသစ်။ လပြည့်	lă*h*, lá*h*-*th*it, lă*h*-byëĕ
moonlight	လသာခြင်း	lă*h* thă*h*-jin:
north	မြောက်	myowk
planet	ဂြိုဟ်	jo*h*
rain	မိုဃ်းရွာခြင်း	mô*h*: yŏŏă*h* jin:

English.	Burmese.	Pronunciation.
rainbow	သတ္တန်	thettá*h*n
shade, shadow	အရိပ်	ă*h*-yayk
sky	မိုဃ်းကောင်းကင်	mô*h*:-kowng:-gin
snow	မိုဃ်းပွင့်	mô*h*:-bwiṇ
south	တောင်	towng
star	ကြယ်	kyeh
sun	နေ	nay
thunder	မိုဃ်းကြိုးခြိမ်း	mô*h*:-chô*h*n:-jin:
water	ရေ	yay
weather	မိုဃ်းလေ	mô*h*:-lay
west	အနောက်	ă*h*-nowk
wind	လေတိုက်ခြင်း	lay-tik-chin:

Land and Water. မြေနှင့်ရေ။

bay	ပင်လယ်ထောင့်ကွေ့	pinleh dowṇg-gwaỵ
beach	ပင်လယ်ကမ်း	pinleh-kă*h*n:
bog	ဇိန့်မြေ	tsayṇ-myay
canal	တူးမြောင်း	too:-myowng:
cape	အငူ	ă*h*-gnoo
cave	ဂူ	koo
chasm	ချောက်	jowk
cliff	ကမ်းစေါက်	kă*h*n:-zowk
coast	ပင်လယ်ကမ်းနား	pinleh-kă*h*n:-nā*h*
creek	ချောင်း	chowng:
current	ရေစီး	yay-żee:
ebb	ရေကျ	yay-jyá*h*
flood (of the tide)	ရေတက်	yay-det
foam	အမြှုပ်	á*h*-hmyo*h*k
forest	တော	taw

English.	Burmese.	Pronunciation.
hill	တောင်	towng
hillock	တောင်ပို့	towng-bo̤*h*
hill-top	တောင်ထိပ်	towng-dayt
ice	ရေခဲ	yay-geh
island	ကျွန်း	kyoon:
lake	အင်း၊ အိုင်	in:, ing
land	ကုန်း	ko*h*n:
marsh	နွန်မြေ	nŏŏn-myay
moor	လွင်ပြင်	lwin-byin
mountain	တောင်ကြီး	towng-jee:
mud	ရွှံ့	shŏŏn
range of hills	ကုန်းတန်း	kô*h*n:-dă*h*n:
range of mountains	တောင်ရိုး	towng-yô*h*:
river	မြစ်	myit
rock	ကျောက်	kyowk
sand	သဲ	theh
sand-bank	သောင်	thowng
sea	ပင်လယ်	pinleh
shingle	ကျောက်စရစ်	kyowk-tsá*h*-yit
spring (water)	ရေစမ်း	yay-tsă*h*n:
storm	မုန်တိုင်း	mo*h*n-ding:
stream	ချောင်း ကလေး	chowng:-gá*h*lay:
tide	ဒီ	dee
valley	ချိုင့်	ching
water, fresh	ရေချို	yay-jo*h*
— salt	ရေငန်	yay-gnä*h*n
waterfall	ရေတံခွန်	yay-tă*h*gŏŏn
water-tank (dug) [reservoir	ရေကန်	yay-gä*h*n
wave	လှိုင်း၊ လှိုင်းထံပိုး	hling:, hling:-tă*h*-bô*h*:

English.	Burmese.	Pronunciation.
well	ရေတွင်း	yay-dwin:
whirlpool	ရေဝဲ	yay-weh:

Minerals and Metals. ဓါတ်သတ္တုနှင့် ကျောက် အမျိုးမျိုး။

English.	Burmese.	Pronunciation.
alum	ကျောက်ချဉ်	kyowk-chin
amber	ပယင်း	pă*h*-yin:
antimony	ခနောက်စိမ်	hkă*h*-nowk-tsayn
arsenic	စိန်	tsayn
borax	လက်ခြား	let-chā*h*:
brass	ကြေးဝါ	kyay:-wā*h*
bricks	အုတ်	o*h*k
bronze	ကြေးနီ	kyay:-nee
cement	အင်္ဂတေ	in:gă*h*day
chalk	မြေဖြူ	myay-byoo
clay	မြေစေး	myay-zee:
coal	ကျောက်မီးသွေး	kyowk-mee:-*th*way:
copper	ကြေးနီ	kyay:-nee
coral	သန္တာ	thă*h*dā*h*
crystal	ကျောက်သလင်း	kyowk-thá*h*lin:
diamond	စိန်ကျောက်	tsayn-jowk
emerald	မြ	myă*h*
flint	မီးခတ်ကျောက်	mee:-gă*h*t-kyowk
glass	ဖန်။ မှန်	hpă*h*n, hmă*h*n
gold	ရွှေ	shway
gravel	ကျောက်စရစ်	kyowk-tsă*h*-yit
iron	သံ	thă*h*n
lead	ခဲမ	hkeh-mă*h*
lime	ထုံးဖြူ	htô*h*n:-byoo
marble	ကျောက်ဖြူ	kyowk-hpyoo

English.	Burmese.	Pronunciation.
mercury	ပြဒါး	pă*h*dā*h*:
mortar	သရွတ်	thă*h*-yŏŏt
opal	မဟူရာ	mă*h*hooyā*h*
ore	သတ္တုကျောက်	thă*h*ttŏŏ-jowk
pearl	ပုလဲ	pă*h*leh
petroleum	ရေနံ	yay-nă*h*n
ruby	ကျောက်နီ	kyowk-nee
salt	ဆား	sā*h*:
sand	သဲ	theh
sapphire	နီလာ	neelā*h*
silver	ငွေ	gnway
soda	ပြာဆား	pyā*h*-zā*h*:
steel	သံမဏိ	thă*h*n-mă*h*nĕĕ
stone	ကျောက်	kyowk
sulphur	ကန့်	kă*h*ŋ
tin	သံဖြူ	thă*h*n-byoo
zinc	သွပ်	thŏŏt

Animals, Birds, and Fishes. သား၊ငှက်၊ငါးအမျိုးမျိုး။

English.	Burmese.	Pronunciation.
animal	သား	thā*h*:
barking deer	ဂျီ	jee
bear	ဝက်ဝံ	wet-wŏŏn
bird	ငှက်	hgnet
buffalo	ကျွဲ	kyŏŏ-eh
bull	နွားထီး	nă*h*-htee:
calf	နွားကလေး	nwā*h*:-gá*h*lay:
cat	ကြောင်	kyowng
chicken	ကြက်ကလေး	kyet-kă*h*lay:
cock	ကြက်ဖ	kyet-hpă*h*

English.	Burmese.	Pronunciation.
colt	မြင်းကလေး	myin:-găhlay:
cow	နွားမ	nwāh:-măh
crab	ဂနန်း။ ပုဇွန်ပြား	găhnăhn:, păhzŏŏn-
crow	ကျီးကန်း	kyee:găhn: [byāh:
dog	ခွေး	hkway:
dove	ချိုး	jôh:
duck	ဝမ်းဘဲ	woom:beh
eagle	ဝံလို	wŏŏnloh
eel	ငါးရှဉ့်	gnāh:-shin
elephant	ဆင်	sin
elk	သမင်	thăhmin
fish	ငါး	gnāh:
fowl	ကြက်	kyet
fox	မြေခွေး	myay-gway:
game	အမဲ	ăh-meh
goat	ဆိတ်	sayt
goose	ငန်းမ။ ငန်းဖို	gnăhn:-măh, (gander)
hare	ယုန်	yohn [gnăhn:-boh
hen	ကြက်မ	kyet-măh, or kyemmăh
hog-deer	ဒရယ်	dăhyeh
hoof	ခွာ	hkwāh
horn	ဦးချို	oo:-joh
horse	မြင်း	myin:
leopard	ကျားသစ်	kyăh-thit
mane	လည်ဆံ	leh-zăhn
mongoose (ichneu-	မြွေပါ	mwaybāh
monkey [mon)	မျောက်	myowk
mouse	ကြွက်	kyŏŏet
mullet	ကဘီလူး	kăh-băhloo:

English.	Burmese.	Pronunciation.
otter	ဖျံ	hpyä*h*n
owl	ငှက်ဆိုး	hgnet-sô*h*:
—, horned	ဒီးဒုတ်	dee:-do*h*k
ox	နွားပြီး	nwā*h*:-byee:
oyster	ကနုကမာ	kă*h*-nŏŏ-kă*h*-mā*h*
parrot	ကျက်တူရွေး	kyet-too-yŏŏay:
partridge	ခါ	hkā*h*
paw	လက်	let
peacock, — hen	ဒေါင်းဖို။ ဒေါင်းမ	downg:-bo*h*, downg:-mă*h*
pheasant	ရစ်	yit
pig	ဝက်	wet
pigeon	ခို	hko*h*
porcupine	ဖြူ	hpyoo
quail	ငုံး	gnô*h*ng:
rabbit	သင်းဘောယုန်	thim:baw-yo*h*n
rat	ကြွက်	kyŏŏet
red deer	ဆတ်	să*h*t
rhinoceros	ကြံ့	kyă*h*n
sheep	သိုး	thô*h*:
snipe	မြေဝပ်	myay-wŏŏt
sparrow	စာကလေး	tsā*h*-gă*h*lay:
starling	ဇရက်	ză*h*-yet
stork	ဗျိုင်းဖြူ	bying:-byoo
swallow	မိုးစွေငှက်၊ ပျံလွှား	mô*h*:-zway-hgnet: pyă*h*n-hlwā*h*:
swan	ရွှေငန်း	shway-gnă*h*n:
tail	အမြီး	ă*h*-myee:
tiger	ကျား	kyā*h*:
tortoise	လိပ်	layk

English.	Burmese.	Pronunciation.
turkey	ငှက်ဆင်	hgnet-sin
turtle	လိပ်။ ပင်လယ် လိပ်	layk, pinleh-layk
vulture	လင်းတ	lá*h*-dá*h*
wild ox	ဆိုင်	tsing
wing	အတောင်	ă*h*-towng
wolf	တောခွေး	taw-gway:

Reptiles and Insects.

လိမ်တွန့်၍သွားသောသားနှင့်ပိုးကောင်များ။

English.	Burmese.	Pronunciation.
ant	ပုရွက်ဆိတ်	pă*h*-yŏŏet-sayt
— (white)	ခြ	chă*h* '
bee	ပျားကောင်	pyā*h*:-gowng
beetle	နောက်ချေးပိုး	nowk-chyëë:-bô*h*:
bug	ကြမ်းပိုး	kyă*h*-bô*h*:
butterfly	လိပ်ပြာ	layk-pyā*h*
caterpillar	ခူ	hkoo
centipede	ကင်းခြေများ	kin:-chëë-myā*h*:
cobra	မြွေဟောက်	mway-howk
crocodile	မိကျောင်း	mëë-jowng:
firefly	ပိုးစိန်းဖြူ	pô*h*:-tsayn:-byoo
flea	ခွေးလှေး	hkway:-hlay:
fly	ယင်ကောင်	yin-gowng
frog	ဖား	hpā*h*:
house lizard	အိမ်မြှောင်	ayn-hmyowng
large house lizard	တောက်တဲ့	towk-teh
insect	ပိုးကောင်	pô*h*:-gowng
leech	ကြွတ် (large) မျှော့	kyŏŏt, hmyaw
mosquito	ခြင်	chin
sand-fly	ဖြုတ်	hpyo*h*k

English.	Burmese.	Pronunciation.
scorpion	ကင်းမြီးကောက်	kin:-myee:-gowk
silkworm	ပိုး	pô*h*:
snake	မြွေ	mway
snake (poisonous)	မြွေဆိုး	mway-zô*h*:
spider	ပင့်ကူ	pin̥-goo
wasp	နကြည်	nă*h*-jeh
worm	တီကောင်	tee-gowng

Fruits, Trees, Flowers, and Vegetables.[1]

အပင်၊အသီး၊ပန်း၊အမျိုးမျိုး ။

almond	ဗါဒါန်	bā*h*dā*h*n
amherstia	သော်က	thāwkă*h*
asparagus	ကညွတ်	kă*h*-nyŏŏt
banana (commonly called 'plantain')	ငှက်ပျော	hgnet-pyaw
banyan	ညောင်	nyowng
beans	ပဲ	peh
beetroot	မုံလာဥနီ	mo*h*n-lā*h*-ŏŏ-nee
bouquet	ပန်းခိုင်	pă*h*n:-ging
cabbage	သင်းဘော မုံလာ	thim:baw mo*h*n-lā*h*
capsicum	ငရုတ်	gnă*h*-yo*h*k
carrot	မုံလာဥဝါ	mo*h*n-lā*h*-ŏŏ-wā*h*
castor-oil plant	ကြက်ဆူ	kyet-soo
citron	ရှောက်သခွါး	showk-thă*h*-hkwā*h*:
cocoa-nut	အုန်း	ô*h*n:
cucumber	သခွါး	thă*h*-hkwā*h*:
custard apple	ဩဇာ	awzā*h*
date	စွန်ပလွံ	tsŏŏmbă*h*lŏŏn

[1] See Note following this list, p. 35.

English.	Burmese.	Pronunciation.
doorian	ဒူးရင်း	doo:-yin:
fern	ကျောက်ပန်း	kyowk-pă*h*n:
fig	သဖန်း	thă*h*-hpă*h*n:
fir (-tree)	ထင်းရှူးပင်	htin:-yoo:-bin
garlic	ကြက်သွန်ဖြူ	kyet-thŏŏn-byoo
grape	စပျစ်	tsă*h*byit
ironwood	ပျင်းကဒိုး	pyin:-gă*h*-dô*h*:
jack	ပိန်းနဲ	payn:-hneh
kernel	အဆန်	ă*h*-să*h*n
leaf	အရွက်	ă*h*-yŏŏet
lemon	ရှောက်ချဉ်	showk-chin
lily (water)	ကြာ	kyā*h*
lime	သံပရာ	thă*h*mbă*h*yā*h*
maize	ပြောင်းဖူး	pyowng:-boo:
mango	သရက်	thă*h*-yet
mulberry	ပိုးစာပင်	pô*h*:-zā*h*-bin
mushroom	မှို	hmo*h*
mustard	မုံညင်း	mo*h*n-nyin:
onion	ကြက်သွန်နီ	kyet-thŏŏn-nee
orange	လိမ်မော်	laymmāw
palmyra (palm)	ထန်း	htă*h*n:
papaya	သင်းဘောသီး	thim:baw-*th*ee:
peas	ပဲ	peh
pepper (black)	ငရုတ်ကောင်း	gnă*h*-yo*h*k-koung:
pine-apple	နနတ်	nă*h*-nă*h*t
plum	ဆီး	zee:
potatoes	မြောက်ဥ	myowk-ŏŏ
pumpkin	ဖရုံ	hpă*h*-yo*h*n
radishes	မုံလာ	mo*h*n-lā*h*

35

English.	Burmese.	Pronunciation.
raisins	စပျစ်သီးခြောက်	tsă*h*-byit-thee:-jowk
rose	နှင်းဆီပန်း	hnin:-zee-bă*h*n:
talipat (palm)	ပေ	pay
tamarind	မန်ကျည်း	mă*h*-jee:
teak	ကျွန်း	kyoon:
tomato	ခရမ်းကျဉ်	hkă*h*-yă*h*n:-jin
water-melon	ဖရဲ	hpă*h*-yeh
willow	မိုဃ်းမခ	mô*h*:-mă*h*-hkă*h*
yam	မျောက်ခေါင်း	myowk-hkowng:

NOTE.—The following list gives the words which must be placed after the name of a plant or tree in order to distinguish the part of the plant to be indicated. Thus, ဆီးပင် *a plum-tree*, ဆီးသီး *a plum*, ဆီးရွက် *a plum-leaf*.

bark	အခေါက်	ă*h*-hkowk
blossom	အပွင့်	ă*h*-pwin̥
branch	အခက်	ă*h*-hket
flower	ပန်း	pă*h*n:
fruit	အသီး	ă*h*-thee:
heart	အနှစ်	ă*h*-hnit
leaf	အရွက်	ă*h*-yŏŏet
plank	ပျဉ်	pyeen
plant	အပင်	ă*h*-pin
root	အမြစ်	ă*h*-myit
seed	အစေ့	ă*h*-tsay̥
shoot	အညွန့်	ă*h*-nyŏŏn̥
sprout	အညှောံ	ă*h*-hnyowk
stalk	အရိုး	ă*h*-yô*h*:
stalk of fruit	အညှာ	ă*h*-hnyā*h*
stump	အငုတ်	ă*h*-gno*h*k

C 2

Colours. အရောင်အဆင်း။

English.	Burmese.	Pronunciation.
black	မည်း၊ နက်	meh:, net
blue	ပြာ	pyā*h*
brown	ညို	nyo*h*
crimson	ရဲရဲနီ	yeh-yeh-nee
dark	ညို	nyo*h*
green	စိမ်း	tsayn:
grey	ဖေါင်းဝတ်	hpowng:-wŏŏt
pink	ပန်းနု	pă*h*n:nŏŏ
red	နီ	nee
scarlet	ထွေးထွေးနီ	htway:-dway:-nee
violet	နီကျင်ကျင်	nee-kyin-jin
white	ဖြူ	hpyoo
yellow	ဝါ	wā

The above are really intransitive verb roots and must be so used. Words implying a tendency towards a colour are formed by prefixing 'khă*h*t' and reduplicating; thus,

ခတ်ဝါဝါ hkă*h*t wā*h*-wā*h*, yellowish.

Times and Seasons. ဥတု၊ လ၊ ရက်၊ နာရီ၊ အချိန်များ။

(For Conversations, see pp. 136–40.)

afternoon	မွန်းလွဲအချိန်	moon:-lweh ă*h*-chayn
beginning	အစ	ă*h*-tsă*h*
century	နှစ်ပေါင်းတရာ	hnit-powng: tă*h*yā*h*
dawn, daybreak	မိုးလင်းစ	mô*h*:-lin:-ză*h*
day (24 hours)	ရက်	yet
day (12 hours)	နေ့	nay
Sunday	တနင်္ဂနွေ	Tă*h*-nin:-gă*h*-nway
Monday	တနင်္လာ	Tă*h*-nin:-lā*h*

English.	Burmese.	Pronunciation.
Tuesday	အင်္ဂါ	In-gā*h*
Wednesday	ဗုဒ္ဓဟူး	Bo*h*k-dă*h*-hoo:
Thursday	ကြာသပတေး	Kyā*h*-thă*h*-bă*h*-day:
Friday	သောက်ကြာ	Thowk-kyā*h*
Saturday	စနေ	Tsă*h*-nay
day after to-morrow	ထံဘက္ခ	thă*h*-bekkă*h*
day before yester- [day	တမျန်နေ့	tă*h*-myă*h*n nąy
daytime	နေ့ အချိန်	nąy ă*h*-chayn
early	စောစော	tsaw-zaw
end	အဆုံး	ă*h*-sô*h*n:
evening	ညနေ	nyă*h*-năy
forenoon	မွန်းမတည့်မှီအချိန်	moon: mă*h*-tei̥-hmee [ă*h*-chayn
fortnight	ဆယ်လေးရက်	seh-lay:-yet
half-an-hour	နာရီတဝက်	nā*h*-yee tă*h*-wet
holiday	ပွဲနေ့	pweh-nąy
hour	နာရီ	nā*h*-yee
last month	လွန်ခဲ့သောလ	lŏŏn-geh̥-*th*aw-lă*h*
last night	မနေ့ည	mă*h*-nąy-nyă*h*
last year	မနှစ်က	mă*h*-hnit-kă*h*
Lent	ဝါ	wā*h*
midnight	သန်းခေါင်	thă*h*-gowng
minute	မိနစ်	mëënit
month	လ	lă*h*
months, English		
January	ဇနဝါရီ	Ză*h*-nă*h*-wā*h*-yee
February	ဖေဘူဝါရီ	Hpay-boo-wā*h*-yee
March	မါတ်	Mā*h*t
April	ဧပရီ	Ay-pă*h*-yee
May	မေ	May

English.	Burmese.	Pronunciation.
June	ဇွန်	Zŏŏn
July	ဇူလိုင်	Zŏŏ-ling
August	ဩဂိုတ်	A*h*-gik
September	စက်တင်ဘာ	Set-tin-bā*h*
October	အောက်တိုးဘာ	Owk-tô*h*:-bā*h*
November	နိုဝင်ဘာ	No*h*-wim-bā*h*
December	ဒီဇင်ဘာ	Dee-sim-bā*h*
months, Burmese[1]		
March	တံခူး	Tá*h*-goo:
April	ကဆုန်	Kă*h*-so*h*n
May	နယုန်	Nă*h*-yo*h*n
June	ဝါဆို	Wā*h*-zo*h*
Intercalary	ဒုတိယဝါဆို	Dŏŏ-tëē-yă*h* Wā*h*-zo*h*
July	ဝါခေါင်	Wā*h*-gowng
August	တော်သလင်း	Tāw-*th*ă*h*-lin:
September	သီတင်းကျွတ်	Thă*h*-din:-jŏŏt
October	တန်ဆောင်မုန်း	Tă*h*-zowng-mô*h*n:
November	နတ်တော်	Nă*h*dāw
December	ပြာသိုထ်	Pyā*h*-*th*o*h*
January	တံပို့တွဲ	Tá*h*-bo*h*-dweh
February	တံပေါင်း	Tă*h*-bowng:
morning	မနက်, *or* နံနက်	mă*h*-net, *or* nă*h*n-net
night	ည	nyă*h*
noon	မွန်းတည့်	moon:-teh
season	ဥတု	ŏŏdŏŏ
—, cold	ဆောင်းဥတု	sowng:-ŏŏdŏŏ
—, hot	နွေဥတု	nway-ŏŏdŏŏ

[1] These months are lunar, and therefore about every third year there is an extra month put in, called Dŏŏtëēyă*h*, or 'second' Wā*h*zo*h*.

English.	Burmese.	Pronunciation.
season, rainy	မိုးဥတု	mô*h*:-ŏŏdŏŏ
second, moment	ခဏ	hkă*h*nă*h*
sunrise	နေထွက်ကာလ	nay-htwet-kā*h*lă*h*
sunset	နေဝင်ကာလ	nay-win-kā*h*lă*h*
time	ကာလ။ အခါ	kā*h*lă*h*, ă*h*-hkā*h*
to-day	ယနေ့	yă*h*-nay
to-morrow	မနက်ဖြန်	mă*h*-net-pyă*h*n
to-night	ယခုည	yă*h*-hkŏŏ-nyă*h*
twilight, dusk	ဝေလီဝေလင်း။ ဆည်း	way-lee-way-lin:, see:-
week (seven days)	ခုနှစ်ရက် [ဆာ	hkŏŏ-hnă*h*-yet [zāh
year	နှစ်	hnit
yesterday	မနေ့	mă*h*-nay
yesterday morning	မနေ့မနက်	mă*h*-nay-mă*h*-net

Town, Country, and Agriculture.

မြို့၊ ရွာနှင့်လယ်လုပ်ရာ အကြောင်း။

bank	မြေရိုး	myay-yô*h*:
bank (edge)	ကမ်း	kă*h*n:
brick house	တိုက်	tik
bridge	တံတား	tă*h*-dā*h*:
building	အဆောင်	ă*h*-sowng
bush, shrub	ချုံ။ ချုံပုတ်	cho*h*n, cho*h*n-bo*h*k
cemetery	သင်းချိုင်း	thin:-jin:
corn	စပါး	tsă*h*-bā*h*:
country, the	ကျေးတော	kyee:-daw [1]
court-house	ရုံး	yo*h*n: [nwā*h*:-yô*h*n
cow-house	နွားတင်းကုပ်။ နွားရုံ	nwā*h*:-tin:-go*h*k,

[1] ကျေ၊ ကြေ၊ ချေ၊ ခြေ are sometimes kyay, chay, and sometimes kyee, chee.

English.	Burmese.	Pronunciation.
crop	လယ်ထွက်	leh-dwet
custom-house	အကောက်တိုက်	ā*h*-kowk-tik
ditch	မြောင်း	myowng:
farm	လယ်ယာ	leh-yā*h*
farmer	လယ်လုပ်သမါး	leh-lo*h*k-thă*h*mā*h*:
fence	ဝင်း။ ခြံ	win:, chă*h*n
field	လယ်ယာ	leh-yā*h*
flock, herd	အစု။ အအုပ်	ă*h*-tsŏŏ, ă*h*-o*h*k
foot-path	ခြေလမ်း	chëë-lă*h*n:
forest	တော	taw
garden	ဥယျာဉ်	ŏŏyin
gate	တန်ခါး	tă*h*-gā*h*:
grass	မြက်ပင်	myet-pin
harvest	စပါးရိတ်ကာလ	tsăh-bā*h*:-yayk-kā*h*lă*h*
hay	မြက်ခြောက်	myet-chowk
hedge	စည်းတန်း	tsee:-dă*h*n:
house (wooden)	အိမ်	ayn
hut	အိမ်ကုတ်။ တဲ	ayn-go*h*k, teh
inn	ထမင်းဆိုင်	htă*h*min:-zing
labourer	ကူလီ။ အလုပ်သမား	koolee, ă*h*-lo*h*k-thă*h*-mā*h*:
land, soil	မြေ	myay
log	သစ်တိုံး	thit-to*h*n:
manure	နောက်ချေး	nowk-chee:
market	ဈေး	zay:
mile	မိုင်	ming
mill	ကြိတ်ဆုံ	kyayt-so*h*n
pagoda	စေတီ။ ဘုရား	zaydee, hpă*h*-yā*h*:
place, spot	အရပ်	ă*h*-yă*h*t
pasture	စားကျက်	tsă*h*-jet

English.	Burmese.	Pronunciation.
plough	ထယ်။ ထွန်တုံး	hteh, htŏŏn-dô*h*n:
police-station	ဌါန့	htā*h*nă*h*
prison	ထောင်	htowng
rice (plant)	ကောက်	kowk
road	လမ်း	lă*h*n:
school	စာသင်ကျောင်း	tsā*h*-*th*in-jowng:
shed	တင်းကုတ်	tin:go*h*k
shop	ဆိုင်	sing
street	အိမ်တန်းလမ်း	ayn-dă*h*n:-lă*h*n:
town	မြို့	myǫ*h*
village	ရွာ	yŏŏā*h*
waterfall	ရေတံခွန်	yay-tă*h*-gŏŏn
wheat	ဂျုံစပါး	jo*h*n-tsă*h*-bā*h*:

Mankind: Relations. လူမျိုး၏တော်စပ်ခြင်း။

aunt	မိကြီး။ မိထွေး။ အရီး	mëë-jee:, mëĕ-dway:, ă*h*-yee:
baby	နို့စို့ကလေး	nǫ*h*-zǫ*h*-gă*h*-lay:
boy	လူကလေး	loo-gă*h*-lay:
brother	ညီ။ အစ်ကို။ မောင်	nyee, itko*h*, mowng[1]
brother-in-law	ယောက်ဖ	yowk-hpă*h*
child	အကလေး။ သူငယ်	ă*h*-kă*h*-lay:, thă*h*-gneh
cousin	ညီတော်။ အစ်ကို[တော်	nyee-dāw, itko*h*-dāw
daughter	သမီး	thă*h*mee:
daughter-in-law	ချွေးမ	chway:-mă*h*
family (lineage)	အမျိုးအနွယ်	ă*h*-myô*h*:-ă*h*-hnweh

[1] မောင် mowng, is used by women to designate a brother, and is also commonly used as a prefix of men's names indicative of equality; thus, မောင်လောက် Mowng Lowk = Mr. Lowk.

English.	Burmese.	Pronunciation.
father	အဖေ။ အဖ။ ဘ။ ခမည်း	ă*h*-hpay, ă*h*-hpă*h*, hbă*h*, hkă*h*-meh:
father-in-law	ယောက္ခမ	yowk-hkă*h*mă*h*
gentleman, Mr.	သခင်။ ခင်ဗြား	thă*h*-hken, hken-byā*h*:
girl	မိန်းကလေး	mayn:-kă*h*lay:
grand-daughter	မြေးမ	myay:-mă*h*
grandfather	အဘိုး။ ဘိုး	ă*h*-hpô*h*:, bô*h*:
grandmother	အဘွား	ă*h*-hpwā*h*:
grandson	မြေး	myay:
husband	လင်	lin
husband's sister	ယောင်းမ	yowng:-mă*h*
lady, Mrs.	သခင်မ။ အရှင်မ။ မယ်။ မမ	thă*h*-hken-ma*h*, ă*h*-shin-mă*h*, meh, mă*h*-mă*h*
maid	အပျို	ă*h*-pyo*h*
man, a	ယောက်ျား	yowk-yā*h*:
man (human being)	လူ	loo
marriage	လက်ထပ်ခြင်း	let-htă*h*t-chin:
married man	အိမ်ထောင်ယောက်ျား	ayn-downg yowk-yā*h*:
married woman	အိမ်ထောင် မိန်းမ	ayn-downg mayn:mă*h*
mother	အမေ။ အမိ	ă*h*-may, ă*h*-mëë
mother-in-law	ယောက္ခမမိန်းမ	yowk-hkă*h*mă*h*-mayn-mă*h*
nephew	တူ	too
niece	တူမ	too-mă*h*
old man	လူအို။ အဘိုးကြီး	loo-o*h*, ă*h*-hpô*h*:-jee:
old woman	အမေကြီး	ă*h*-may-jee:
parents	မိဘ	mëëbă*h*
people	သူများ	thoo-myā*h*:
person [or	သူ	thoo
single man, bachel-	လူပျို	loo-byo*h*

English.	Burmese.	Pronunciation.
single woman	အပျို	ă*h*-pyo*h*
young lady, Miss	မိရှင်။	mee-shin
sister	အစ်မ။ ညီမ	ă*h*-mă*h*, nyee-mă*h*
sister-in-law	ခယ်မ။ ယောင်းမ	hkeh-mă*h*, yowng:-[ma*h*
son	သား	thā*h*:
son-in-law	သားမက်	thā*h*-met
step-father	ဘထွေး	bă*h*-dway:
step-mother	မိထွေး	meë-dway:
step-son	အထက်သား	ă*h*-htet-thā*h*:
uncle	ဘကြီး။ ဘထွေး။	bă*h*-jee:, bă*h*-dway:
widow	မုဆိုးမ	mo*h*k-sô*h*:-mă*h*
widower	မုဆိုးဖို	mo*h*k-sô*h*:-bo*h*
wife	မယား	mă*h*-yā*h*:
wife's sister	ခယ်မ	hkeh-mă*h*
woman	မိန်းမ	mayn:-mă*h*

The Human Body. လူ၏အင်္ဂါများ။

English.	Burmese.	Pronunciation.
ankle	ဖမျက်	hpă*h*-myet
arm	လက်မောင်း	let-mowng:
back	ကျောကုန်း	kyaw-gô*h*n:
beard	မုဆိတ်	mŏŏ-sayt *or* mo*h*k-[sayt
blood	သွေး	thway:
body	ကိုယ်ကာယ	ko*h*-kā*h*yă*h*
bone	အရိုး	ă*h*-yô*h*:
bowels	အူ	oo
brain	အနှောက်	ô*h*n:-hnowk
cheek	ပါး	pā*h*:
chest	ရင်ပတ်	yin-ba*h*t
chin	မေးစေ့	may:-zeȩ

English.	Burmese.	Pronunciation.
complexion	အရောင် အဆင်း	ă*h*-yowng ă*h*-sin:
ear	နား၊ နားရွက်	nā*h*:, nă*h*-yŏŏet
elbow	တံတောင်ဆစ်	tă*h*-downg-zit
eye	မျက်စိ	myet-tsēē
face	မျက်နှာ	myet-hnā*h*
finger	လက်ချောင်း	let-chowng:
flesh	အသား	ă*h*-thā*h*:
foot	ခြေ	chyay, *or* chee
forehead	နဖူး	nă*h*-hpoo:
hair (of head)	ဆံပင်	să*h*-bin
hand	လက်	let
head	ဦးခေါင်း၊ ခေါင်း	o*h*k-hkowng:, gowng:
heart	နှစ်လုံး	hnit-lô*h*n: *or* hnă*h*-lô*h*n:
heel	ခြေဖနှောင့်	chyay-hpă*h*-hnowng
jaw	ပါးချိတ်ရိုး	pā*h*-chayt-yô*h*:
joint	အဆက်၊ အဆစ်	ă*h*-set, ă*h*-sit
kidneys	ကျောက်ကပ်	kyowk-kă*h*t
knee	ဒူး	doo:
leg	ခြေထောက်	chyay-dowk
limb	ကိုယ်အင်္ဂါ	ko*h*-ingā*h*
lip	နှုတ်ခမ်း	hnă*h*-hkă*h*n:
liver	အသည်း	ă*h*-theh:
lungs	အဆုတ်	ă*h*-so*h*k
moustache	နှုတ်ခမ်းမွေး	hnă*h*-hkă*h*n:-mway:
mouth	ပစပ်၊ ခံတွင်း	pă*h*-ză*h*t, hkă*h*-dwin:
nail	လက်သည်း	let-theh:
neck	လည်ပင်း	leh-bin:
nose	နှာခေါင်း	hnā*h*-hkowng:

English.	Burmese.	Pronunciation.
rib	နံရိုး	năhn-yôh:
shoulder	ပခုံး	păh-hkôhn:
side	နံဘေး	năh-bay:
skin	အရေ။ သားရေ	ăh-yay, thăh-yay
skull	ဥခေါင်းခွံ	ohk-hkowng:-gŏŏn
spine	ကျောရိုး	kyaw-yôh:
thigh	ပေါင်လုံး	powng-lôhn:
throat	လည်ချောင်း	leh-jowng:
thumb	လက်မ	let-măh
toe	ခြေချောင်း	chyay-jowng:
tongue	လျှာ	shāh
tooth	သွား	thwāh:
whiskers	ပါးမွေး	pāh-mway:
wrist	လက်ဆစ်	let-sit

Physical and Mental Powers, Qualities, &c.

ဉာဏ်သတ္တိဂုဏ်ကျေးဇူးများ။

English.	Burmese.	Pronunciation.
age	အသက်အရွယ်	ăh-thet-ăh-yŏŏeh
— old	အသက်ကြီးခြင်း	ăh-thet-kyee:-jin:
anger	အမျက်။ ဒေါသ	ăh-myet, dawthăh
art	အတတ်ပညာ	ăh-tăht-pëënyāh
breadth, width	အနံ။ ဗြက်	ăh-năhn, byet
character (good)	အသရေ	ăh-thăh-yay
childhood	သူငယ်အဖြစ်	thoo-gneh-ăh-hpyit
depth	နက်ခြင်း	net-chin:
dislike	မနှစ်သက်ခြင်း	măh-hnit-thet-chin:
disposition	သဘော	thăhbaw
fear	စိုးရိမ်ခြင်း	tsôh:-yayn-jin:
foolishness, folly	မောဟ။ မိုက်ခြင်း	mawhăh, mik-chin:

English.	Burmese.	Pronunciation.
gentleness	သိမ်မွေ့ခြင်း	thayn-mwa̤y-jin:
goodness	ကောင်းခြင်း	kowng:-jin:
greatness	ကြီးခြင်း	kyee:-jin:
hatred	မုန်းခြင်း	mo*h*n:-jin:
height	ကိုယ်အရပ်မြင့်ခြင်း	ko*h*-ă*h*-yă*h*t-myin̤-jin:
honesty	စိတ်ဖြောင့်ခြင်း	tsayt-hpyowng̤-jin:
honour	ဂုဏ်အသရေရှိခြင်း	go*h*n-ă*h*thă*h*yay-shëë-[jin:
intelligence	ဉာဏ်	nyā*h*n
joy	ဝမ်းမြောက်ခြင်း	woon:-myowk-chin:
judgment (faculty)	ဆင်ခြင်ရန်သတ္တိ	sin-jin-yă*h*n-thă*h*ttëë
knowledge	သိပ္ပံအတတ်	thayppă*h*n-ă*h*-tă*h*t
laughter, a laugh	ရယ်ခြင်း	yeh-jin:
length	အရှည်၊ အလျား	ă*h*-shay, ă*h*-lyā*h*:
love	ချစ်ခြင်း	chit-chin:
mind	စိတ်	tsayt
patience	သည်းခံခြင်း	thee:-hkă*h*n-jin:
pleasure	ပျော်မွေ့ခြင်း	pyāw-mwa̤y-jin:
politeness, courtesy	ပျူငှါ။ လောကဝတ် [ဉာဏ်	pyoo-hgnā*h*, law-kă*h*-wŏŏt [nyā*h*n
reason (faculty)	ဆင်ခြင်တတ်သော	sin-jin-dă*h*t-thaw-
science	အတတ်ပညာ	ă*h*-tă*h*t-pëënyā*h*
senses, the	ဝေဒနာ	waydă*h*nā*h*
feeling, touch	တွေ့ခြင်း	twa̤y-jin:
hearing	နားကြားခြင်း	nā*h*:-kyā*h*:-jin:
seeing, sight	မြင်ခြင်း	myin-jin:
smelling, smell	နမ်းခြင်း	nă*h*n:-jin:
tasting, taste	မြည်းစမ်းခြင်း	myee:-ză*h*n:-jin:
shape	ပုံသဏ္ဌာန်	po*h*n-thă*h*dā*h*n
size	ဒုဒယ်	dŏŏdeh

English.	Burmese.	Pronunciation.
smell (odour)	အနံ့	ăh-năhn̥
smiling, a smile	ပြုံးခြင်း	pyôhn:-jin:
sneezing, a sneeze	ချေခြင်း	chee-jin:
sorrow	စိတ်ပူခြင်း	tsayt-poo-jin:
speaking, speech	ပြောခြင်း။ စကား	pyaw-jin:, tsăh-gāh:-
strength	ခွန်အား [ပြောချက်	hkŏŏn-āh: [pyaw-jet
stupidity	ညာဏ်ထုံးခြင်း	nyāhn-tôhn:-jin:
surprise	အံ့အောခြင်း	ăhn̥-aw-jin:
taste (of a thing)	အရသာ	ăhyăhthăh
thickness	ဒု	dŏŏ
thinking, thought	ထင်မှတ်ခြင်း	htin-hmăht-chin:
thought, a	စိတ်ထင်ခြက်	tsayt-htin-jet
voice	အသံ	ăh-thăhn
weakness (quality)	အားနည်းခြင်း	āh:-neh:-jin:
wisdom	ပညာ	pëenyāh
youth (quality)	ပျိုသောအရွယ်	pyoh-thaw-ăh-yŏŏeh

Health. ကျန်းမာခြင်း။

abscess	အိုင်နာ	ing-nāh [chin:
accident	မထောင်တဆဖြစ်ခြင်း	măh-tāw tăh-săh hpyit
ague	တုန်ဖျားနာ	tohn-byāh:-nāh
ambulance	လူနာဆောင်ရာ	loo-nāh sowng-yāh
aperient	ဝမ်းနှုတ်ဆေး	woon:-hnohk-say:
asthma	ပန်းနာ	păhn:-nāh
bandage	ကြပ်စည်းရာ	kyăht-tsee:-yāh
biliousness	သည်းခြေနာ	theh:-jee-nāh
blister (of the skin)	အဖေါင်း	ăh-hpowng:
boil	အနာစိမ်း	ăh-năh-zayn:
bruise	အသားကြေနာ	ăh-thăh-jay-nāh

English.	Burmese.	Pronunciation.
burn	မီးလောင်နာ	mee:-lowng-nā*h*
cancer	အနာဆိုး	ă*h*-nă*h*-zô*h*:
chemist's (shop)	ဆေးဆိုင်	say:-zing
chicken-pox	ကျောက်ဖြူနာ	kyowk-hpyoo-nā*h*
cholera	ကာလနာ ရောဂါ	kā*h*lă*h*-nā*h* yawgā*h*
cold	နှာစေးနာ	hnā*h*-zay:-nā*h*
contagion	အနာကူးခြင်း	ă*h*-nā*h*-koo:-jin:
cough	ချောင်းဆိုးနာ	chowng:-zô*h*:-nā*h*
cramp	ညောင်းညာခြင်း	nyowng:-nyā*h*-jin:
diarrhœa	ဝမ်းကျနာ	woon:-jă*h*-nā*h*
disease, illness	အနာရောဂါ	ă*h*-nā*h*-yawgā*h*
doctor, physician	ဆေးသမား	say:-thă*h*mā*h*:
dysentery	သွေးပါဝမ်းကျနာ	thway:-bā*h*-woon:-jă*h*-nā*h*
exhaustion	အား ကုံခြင်း	ā*h*:-ko*h*n-jin:
faint, to	မိန်းမောသည်	mayn:-maw-*th*ëë
fever	ဖျားနာ	hpyā*h*:-nā*h*
fit	တက်နာ	tet-nā*h*
fracture	အရိုးကျိုးခြင်း	ă*h*-yô*h*:-kyô*h*:-jin:
headache	ခေါင်းကိုက်နာ	gowng:-kik-nā*h*
hospital	သူနာတန်	thoo-nā*h*-dă*h*n
ill, sick, to be	နာသည်	nā*h*-*th*ëë
indigestion	အစားမကြေခြင်း	ă*h*-tsā*h*: mă*h*-kyay-jin:
inflammation	အသားပူခြင်း	ă*h*-thā*h*:-poo-jin:
insanity	အရူးနာ	ă*h*-yoo:-nā*h*
itch	ယားနာ	yā*h*:-nā*h*
lameness	ခြေမစွမ်းခြင်း	chyay mă*h*-tsoon:-jin:
leprosy	နူနာ	noo-nā*h*
measles	ဝက်သက်နာ	wet-thet-nā*h*
medicine	ဆေးဝါး	say:-wā*h*:

English.	Burmese.	Pronunciation.
nurse	လူနာထိန်း	loo-nā*h*-dayn:
ointment	ဖယောင်းချက်	hpă*h*-yowng:-jet
pain	နာခြင်း	nā*h*-jin:
paralysis	လေကြောသေနာ	lay-jaw-thay-nā*h*
piles	မြင်းသရိုက်နာ	myin:-thă*h*-yik-nā*h*
pill	ဆေးလုံး	say:-lô*h*n:
poison	အဆိပ်	ă*h*-sayt
prescription	ဆေးပညတ်	say:-pĕĕnyat
quinsey	အုံးလွှဲနာ	ô*h*n:-lweh-nā*h*
rheumatism	တူလာနာ	doo-lā*h*-nā*h*
ringworm	ပွေးနာ	pway:-nā*h*
scald	ရေပူလောင်ခြင်း	yay-boo-lowng-jin:
sickness	အန်ခြင်း	ă*h*n-jin:
smallpox	ကျောက်ပေါက်နာ	kyowk-powk-nā*h*
sprain	အကြောမြက်ခြင်း	ă*h*-kyaw-myet-chin:
tonic	အားတိုးဆေး	ā*h*:-tô*h*:-zay:
unwell, to be	မမါသည်	mă*h*-mā*h*-*th*ĕĕ
well, to be	မါသည်	mā*h*-*th*ĕĕ
wound	အနာအဆာ	ă*h*-nā*h* ă*h*-sā*h*

Food, Drink, and Smoking. အစာအသောက်များ။

(For Conversations, see p. 132.)

English.	Burmese.	Pronunciation.
appetite	စားသောက်ရန်သ	tsā*h*: thowk-yă*h*n thă*h*-
beverages	သောက်စရာ [ဘော	thowk-tsă*h*-yā*h* [baw
beer	ဂျုံရည်	jo*h*n-yĕĕ
coffee	ကာဖီရည်	kā*h*-hpĕĕ-yĕĕ
lemonade	ရှောက်ချဉ်ရည်ဖျော်	showk - chin - yĕĕ -
milk	နို့ရည်	no*h*-yĕĕ [hpyāw
—, of cows	နွားနို့	nă*h*-no*h*
soda-water	ဗိလတ်ရေ	bĕĕlă*h*t-yay

English	Burmese.	Pronunciation.
tea	လက်ဖက်ရည်	láh-hpet-yëë
water	ရေ	yay
wine	စပျစ်ရည်	tsă*h*-byit-yĕŏ
bread	မုန့်။ — ပေါင်မုန့်	mo*h*n,—powng:-mo*h*n
boil, to	ပြုတ်သည်	pyo*h*k-thëë
bottle	ပုလင်း	pă*h*lin:
butter	ထောပတ်	htawbă*h*t
cake	မုန့်ချို	mo*h*n-jo*h*
cheese	ဒိန်ခဲ	dayn-geh
chicken flesh	ကြက်သား	kyet-thā*h*:
cinnamon	သစ်ကျံပိုး	thit-kyă*h*-bô*h*:
cook, to	ချက်သည်	chet-théĕ
cream	နို့ဆီ	no*h*-zee
curd	နို့ခဲ	no*h*-geh
curry	ဟင်း	hin:
eggs	ကြက် ဥ	kyet ŏŏ
fish, dried	ငါးခြောက်	gnă*h*:-jowk
—, fresh	ငါးစိမ်း	gnă*h*:-zayn:
flour	မုန့်ညက်	mo*h*n-nyet
fruits	အသီးများ	ă*h*-thee:-myā*h*:
fry, to	ကြော်သည်	kyāw-*th*ëĕ
ginger	ချင်းစိမ်း	jin:-zayn:
honey	ပျားရည်	pyā*h*:-yee
hungry, to be	ဆာမွတ်သည်	sā*h*-mŏŏt-thëĕ
ice	ရေခဲ	yay-geh
jam	ယို	yo*h*
meals[1] (cooked food)	အနပ်	ă*h*-nă*h*t

[1] Breakfast, lunch, and supper are simply morning, afternoon, and night meals, but the word အစာ ă*h*-tsā*h* is used instead of အနပ်.

English.	Burmese.	Pronunciation.
breakfast	နံနက်စာ	nă*h*net-tsā*h*
luncheon	မွန်းလွဲစာ	moon:-lweh-zā*h*
supper	ညစာ	nyă*h*-zā*h*
meat	အသား	ă*h*-thā*h*:
beef	နွားသား	nwā*h*:-*th*ā*h*:
fat	အဆီ	ă*h*-see
kidneys	ကျောက်ကပ်	kyowk-kă*h*t
mutton	သိုးသား	thô*h*:-*th*ā*h*:
pork	ဝက်သား	wet:-thā*h*:
veal	နွားကလေးသား	nwā*h*:-gă*h*lay:-*th*ā*h*:
mustard	မုံညင်း	mo*h*n-nyin:
nutmegs	ဇာတိပ္ဖိုလ်သီး	zā*h*daykhpo*h*-*th*ee:
oil	ဆီ	see
pepper, black	ငရုတ်ကောင်း	gnă*h*-yo*h*k-kowng:
—, red	ငရုတ်	gnă*h*-yo*h*k
pickles	သနပ်	thă*h*-nă*h*t
pudding	မုန့်ဖျော့	mo*h*n-byaw
rice, boiled	ထမင်း	htă*h*-min:
rice, unboiled	ဆန်	să*h*n
roast, to	ကင်သည်	kin-*th*ĕĕ
salt	ဆား	sā*h*:
sauce	စမဲ	tsă*h*-meh
smoking	ဆေးသောက်ခြင်း	say:-thowk-chin:
cigar	ဆေးလိပ်	say:-layk
matches	မီးချစ်	mee:-jit
pipe	ဆေးတန်	say:-dă*h*n
tobacco	ဆေး	say:
tobacco-pouch	ဆေးအိတ်	say:-ayk
soup	အပြုတ်ရည်	ă*h*-pyo*h*k-yĕĕ

English.	Burmese.	Pronunciation.
spirits	အရက်	ă*h*-yet
sugar	သကြား	thă*h*-jā*h*:
thirst	ရေငတ်ခြင်း	yay-gnă*h*t-chin:
tooth-pick	သွားကြားဒုတ်	thwā*h*:-jā*h*:-do*h*k
under-done, to be	မကျက်တကျက်ရှိ [သည်	mă*h*-kyet-tă*h*-jet-[shĕĕ-*th*ĕĕ
vegetables	ဟင်းရွက်	hin:-yuet
venison	ဒရယ်သား	dă*h*-yeh-*th*ā*h*:
vinegar	ပုံးရည်	pô*h*n:-yĕĕ
well-done, to be	ကျက်သည်	kyet-thĕĕ

Cooking and Table Utensils.

ကျက်ပြုတ်ရန် အသုံးအဆောင်။

(For Conversations, see pp. 132, 145.

basin	ဇလုံပုကန်	ză*h*-lô*h*n-pă*h*-gă*h*n
canister	သံဖြူပုံး	thă*h*n-byoo-bô*h*n:
coffee-pot	ကာဖီခရား	kā*h*-hpee-hkă*h*-yā*h*:
corkscrew	ဝက်အူ	wet-oo
cup	ခွက်	hkwet
dish	ပုကန်ပြားကြီး	pă*h*-gă*h*n-byā*h*:-jee:
dish-cover	ပုကန်အုပ်	pă*h*-gă*h*n-o*h*k
filter	ရေစစ်	yay-zit
fork	ခက်ရင်း	hkă*h*-yin:
glass, tumbler	ဖန်ကတုန်း	hpă*h*n-gă*h*-dô*h*n:
jar	စဉ့်အိုး	tsin-ô*h*:
jug	ခရား	hkă*h*-yā*h*:
kettle	ရေနွေးအိုး	yay-nway:-ô*h*:
knife	ဓား	dā*h*:
ladle	ယောက်ချို	yowk-cho*h*
lamp	မီးအိမ်	mee:-ayn

English.	Burmese.	Pronunciation.
lid	အဖုံး	ă*h*-hpô*h*n:
mat	ဖျာ	hpyā*h*
mortar	ဆုံး	sô*h*n:
oven	ပေါင်းဖို	powng:-bo*h*
pail	ရေပုန်း	yay-bô*h*n:
pestle	ကျည်ပွေ့	kyă*h*-bwĝy
plate	ပုကန်ပြား	pă*h*-gă*h*n-byā*h*:
salt-cellar	ဆားခွက်	sā*h*:-gwet
saucepan	ဒယ်အိုး	deh-ô*h*:
scales	ချိန်ခွင်	chayn-gwin
serviette	လက်သုတ်ပဝါ	let-tho*h*k-pă*h*-wā*h*
sieve	ဆန်ခါ	să*h*-gā*h*
spoon	ဇွန်း	zoon:
strainer	စစ်အိုး	tsit-ô*h*:
table-cloth	စားပွဲခင်း	tsă*h*-bweh-gin:
teapot	လက်ဖက်ရည်ခရား	lă*h* - hpet - yëë - hkă*h* - yā*h*:
tray	လင်ပန်း	lim-bă*h*n:
water-bottle	ရေပလင်း	yay-pă*h*-lin:
wine-glass	ဖန်ကတိုးခြေထောက်	hpă*h*n-gă*h*-dô*h*n:-chyay-dowk

Dress and the Toilet. အဝတ်ထန်ဆာ နှင့် ဆင်ရင်ခြင်း။

(For Shopping, see p. 145.)

bath (room)	ရေချိုးခန်း	yay-chô*h*:-gă*h*n:
bootlaces	ဖိနပ်ကြိုး	hpă*h*-nă*h*t-kyô*h*:
boots	ဘွတ်ဖိနပ်	bŏŏt-hpă*h*-nă*h*t
bracelet	လက်ကောက်	let-kowk
braces	ဘောင်းဘီကြိုးပြား	bowmbee kyô*h*:-byā*h*
breeches	ဘောင်းဘီတို	bowmbee-do*h*

English.	Burmese.	Pronunciation.
brush	ဝက်မှင်ဘီး	wet-hmin-bee:
brush, nail-	လက်သည်းဘီး	let-theh:-bee:
—, tooth-	သွားတိုက်တံပွတ်	thwā*h*:·tik-tă*h*-bŏŏt
buckle	ထိကပေါက်	tée-gă*h*-bowk
button	ကြယ်သီး	kyeh-*th*ee:
button-hook	ကြယ်သီးကောက်	kyeh-thee:-gowk
cap	ဦးထုပ်	o*h*k-hto*h*k
cloak	ဝတ်လုံအင်္ကျီ	wŏŏt-lo*h*n-in:jee
clothing, dress	အဝတ်	ă*h*-wŏŏt
coat	အင်္ကျီ	injee
collars	လည်ပတ်	leh-bă*h*t
comb	ဘီး	bee:
corsets, stays	ကိုယ်ကျတ်အင်္ကျီ	ko*h*-jă*h*t-in:jee
drawers	ခြေးခံပေါင်းဘီ	chway:-gă*h*n-bowm:-
dress, gown	ဂါကရာ	gā*h*gă*h*yā*h* [bee
eye-glasses	မျက်မှန်	myet-hmă*h*n
frock-coat	အင်္ကျီရှည်	in:jee-shay
garters	ခြေစွပ်စည်းကြိုး	chay-zŏŏt tsee:-jô*h*:
gloves	လက်စွပ်	let-tsŏŏt
handkerchief	လက်ကိုင်ပဝါ	let-king-bă*h*· wā*h*
hat	သိုးဦးထုပ်	thô*h*:-o*h*k-hto*h*k
jacket	အင်္ကျီခါးတို	in:jee-hkă*h*-do*h*
jewellery	တန်ဆာ	tă*h*-zā*h*
linen [ror	ပိုက်ဆန်အထည်	piksă*h*n-ă*h*-hteh
looking-glass, mir-	မှန်	hmă*h*n
material(dress,&c.)	အထည်အလိပ်	á*h*-hteh ă*h*-layk
calico	ပိတ်	payt
cloth	သက္ကလတ်	thă*h*gă*h*lă*h*t
flannel	သက္ကလတ်	thă*h*gă*h*lă*h*t

English.	Burmese.	Pronunciation.
fur	သားမွေး	thā*h*:-mway:
lace	ဇာနု	zā*h*-nŏŏ
leather	သားရေ	thă*h*-yăy
muslin	လေလူဇာ	lay-loo-zā*h*
satin	ဖဲ	hpeh
silk	ပိုး	pô*h*:
velvet	ကတ္တီပါ	kă*h*deebā*h*
wool	သိုးမွေး	thô*h*:-mway:
needle	အပ်	ă*h*t
overcoa	ပြင်အင်္ကျီ	pyin-in:jee
parasol	ထီး	htee:
petticoat	ထမိန်။ လုံချည်	htă*h*mayn, lo*h*n-jĕĕ
pins	တွယ်အပ်	tweh-ă*h*t
pocket	အိတ်	ayk
pocket-book	မှတ်စာအုပ်	hmă*h*t-tsā*h*-o*h*k
purse	သားရေအိတ်	thă*h*-yay-ayk
pyjamas, jacket	ညအိပ်အင်္ကျီ	nyă*h*-ayk-in:jee
— trousers	ညအိပ်ဘောင်းဘီ	nyă*h*-ayk-bowmbee
razor	သင်တုန်း	thin-dô*h*n:
ribbon	ပိုးကြိုးပြား	pô*h*:-kyô*h*:-byā*h*:
ring	လက်စွပ်	let-tsŏŏt
scissors	ကတ်ကြေး	kă*h*t-kyĕĕ:
shawl	တပက်	tă*h*-bet
shirt	ကမ္ဘီဇာ	kă*h*mbeezā*h*
shoes	ခြေနင်း	chee-nin:
skirt	လုန်ချည်	lo*h*n-jĕĕ
sleeve	အင်္ကျီလက်	in:jĕĕ-let
slippers	ရှေ့ထိုးဖိနပ်	shay-dô*h*:-pă*h*-nă*h*t
soap	ဆပ်ပြာ	satpyā*h*

English.	Burmese.	Pronunciation.
socks	ခြေစွပ်	chee-zŏŏt
spectacles	မျက်မှန်	myet-hmă*h*n
sponge	ရေမှို	yay-hmo*h*
stockings	ခြေစွပ်ရှည်	chee-zŏŏt-shay
stud	အသီး။ ကြယ်သီး	ă*h*-thee:, kyeh-*th*ee:
suit (clothes)	အဝတ်စုံ	ă*h*-wŏŏt-tso*h*n
tape	ကျပ်ကြိုးပြား	jă*h*t-kyô*h*:-byā*h*:
thimble	အချုပ်လက်စွပ်	ă*h*-cho*h*k-let-tsŏŏt
thread	ချည်	chĕĕ
tie, neck-tie	လည်ကြိုး	leh-jyô*h*:
tooth-powder	သွားတိုက်မှုန့်	thwā*h*:-tik-hmo*h*n
towel	လက်သုတ်ပဝါ	let-tho*h*k-pă*h*-wā*h*
trousers	ပေါင်းဘီ	bowmbee
tunic	ကိုယ်ကျပ်အင်္ကျီ	ko*h*-kyă*h*t-in:jee
turban	ခေါင်းပေါင်း	gowng:-bowng:
umbrella	ထီးလက်	htee:-let
undervest	ချွေးခံအင်္ကျီ	chway:-gă*h*n-in:jee
veil	မျက်နှာဖုံး	myet-hnā*h*-hpô*h*n:
waist cloth (native)	ပုဆိုး	pă*h*-sô*h*:
waistcoat	လက်တိုအင်္ကျီ	let-to*h*-in:jee
walking-stick	ဒုတ်	do*h*k
watch	နာရီခွက်	nā*h*-yee-gwet
waterproof (coat)	ရေမစွတ်အင်္ကျီ	yay-mă*h*-tsŏŏt-in:jee

The House and Furniture. အိမ်တွင်အသုံးအဆောင်။

(For Shopping, see p. 145.)

apartment	အိမ်ခန်း	ayn-gă*h*n:
armchair	ကုလားထိုင်ရှည်	kă*h*lă*h*-hting-shay
bathroom	ရေချိုးခန်း	yay-chô*h*:-gă*h*n:

English.	Burmese.	Pronunciation.
beam	ရောက်။ ထုပ်။ ကြား	yowk, hto*h*k, kyā*h*:-
bedclothes	အိပ်ရာခင်း [မော့	ayk-yā*h*-gin: [maw
bedroom	အိပ်ရာခန်း	ayk-yā*h*-gă*h*n:
bedstead, bed	ခုတင်	hkă*h*-din
blanket	သက္ကလတ်စောင်	thă*h*gă*h*lă*h*t-tsowng
blind	အကွယ်အကာ	ă*h*-kweh-ă*h*-kā*h*
bolster	ခေါင်းအုံးရှည်	gowng:-ô*h*n:-shay
bolt	မင်းထုပ်	min:-do*h*k
book	စာအုပ်	tsā*h*-o*h*k
box	သစ်တာ	thit-tā*h*
brick	အုတ်	ô*h*k
broom	တန်မြက်စည်း	tă*h*-byet-tsĕĕ:
candle	ဖယောင်းတိုင်	hpă*h*-yowng:-ding
candlestick	ဖယောင်းတိုင်ခုံ	hpă*h*-yowng:-ding-
carpet	ကော်ဇော	kāw-zaw [go*h*n
ceiling	မျက်နှာကြက်	myet-hnă*h*-jet
chair, seat	ကုလားထိုင်	kăhlă*h*-hting
chest of drawers	အံထိုးသစ်တာ။ မတ် တတ်သစ်တာ	a*h*n-dô*h*:-thittā*h*, mă*h*t- tă*h*t-thittā*h*
clock	မတ်တတ်နာရီ	mă*h*t-tă*h*t nā*h*-yee
couch	လျောင်းရာခုတင်	lyowng:-yā*h*-hkă*h*-din
counterpane	တင်းတိမ်	tin:-dayn
cradle	ပုခက်	pă*h*-hket
curtain	ကုလားကာ	kă*h*lă*h*-gā*h*
cushion	မှီအုံး။ ဖုံ	hmee-ô*h*n:, hpo*h*n
dining-room	ထမင်းစားခန်း	htă*h*-min:-zā*h*:-gă*h*n:
door	တံခါး	tă*h*-gā*h*:
door-way	တံခါးပေါက်	tă*h*-gă*h*-bowk
— (leaf)	တံခါးရွက်	tă*h*-gă*h*-yŏŏet

English.	Burmese.	Pronunciation.
door-sill	တံခါးခုံ	tă*h*-gă*h*-hko*h*n
eaves	အမိုးစွန်း	ă*h*-mô*h*:-zoon:
floor	ကြမ်း	kyă*h*n:
storey	အိမ်ဆင့်။ အဆင့်	ayn-ziņ, ă*h*-siņ
garden	ဥယျာဉ်	ŏŏ-yin
grate	မီးဖို	mee:-bo*h*
hall (entrance)	ဝင်ခန်း	win-gă*h*n:
hand-basin	ဇလုံ။ အင်တုံ	ză*h*-lô*h*n, in-do*h*n
hinge	ပတ္တာ	pă*h*ttā*h*
house	အိမ်။	ayn
—, brick or stone	တိုက်	tik
key	သော့	thaw
kitchen	ထမင်းချက်ရုံ	htă*h*-min:-jet-yo*h*n
lamp	မီးအိမ်	mee:-ayn
latch	တံခါးကျင်	tă*h*-gă*h*-jin
lock	သော့အိမ်	thaw-ayn
mat	ဖျာ	hpyā*h*
mattress	မွေ့ရာ	mway-yā*h*
mirror	မှန်	hmă*h*n
mosquito-curtains	ခြင်ထောင်	chin-downg
padlock	သော့ခလောက်	thaw-gă*h*-lowk
piano	စန်းဒယား	tsä*h*n:-dú*h*-yā*h*:
picture	ရုပ်ပုန်	*y*o*h*k-po*h*n
pillar	ကျောက်တိုင်	kyowk-ting
pillow	ခေါင်းအုံး	gowng:-ô*h*n:
post	သစ်တိုင်	thit-ting
punkah	ရပ်တောင်	yă*h*t-towng
quilt	စောင်	tsowng
rafters (bamboo)	အခြင်	ă*h*-chin

English.	Burmese.	Pronunciation.
rafters (wood)	ရနယ်	yă*h*-neh
roof	အမိုး	ă*h*-mô*h*:
room	အခန်း	ă*h*-hkă*h*n:
screen	ကုလားကာ	kă*h*lă*h*-gā*h*
sideboard	မတ်တတ်သစ်ထာ	mă*h*t-tă*h*t-thittā*h*
smoke	မီးခိုး	mee:-gô*h*:
sofa	သာလွန်	thā*h*-lŏŏn
soot	ကြပ်ခိုး	kyă*h*t-hkô*h*:
spark	မီးပေါက်	mee:-bowk
stairs, steps	လှေကား	hlay-gā*h*:
table	စားပွဲ	tsā*h*-bweh
thatch	သက်ကယ်။ ဓနိဖက်	thekkeh, dă*h*nĕĕ-bet
tile (of roof)	အုပ်ကြွတ်	o*h*k-kyŏŏt
vase	ဖန်ဖလား	hpă*h*n hpă*h*-lā*h*:
verandah	ခလောက်ဆွဲ	hkă*h*-lowk-sweh
wall	တံတိုင်း။ နံရံ	tă*h*-ding:, nă*h*n-yă*h*n
water-closet (w.c.)	ရေအိမ်	yay-ayn
window	ပြတင်းပေါက်	pă*h*-din:-bowk
writing-desk	စာရေးခုံ	tsā*h*-yay:-go*h*n

Professions and Trades. လက်မှုပညာအတတ်များ။

(For Shopping, &c., see p. 145.)

English.	Burmese.	Pronunciation.
actor	ဇာတ်သမား	zā*h*t-thă*h*mā*h*:
ambassador	သံတမန်	thă*h*n-tă*h*-mă*h*n
architect	ဗိသုကာဆရာ	payttă*h*gā*h*-să*h*yā*h*
attorney	ရှေ့နေ	shay-nay
baker	မုန့်သည်	mo*h*n-*th*eh
banker	ဘဏ်လိုက်စိုး	bă*h*n-tik-tsô*h*:
barber	ဆတ္တာသည်	sattā*h*-*th*eh

English.	Burmese.	Pronunciation.
blacksmith	ပန်းပဲ	pă*h*-beh
boatman, head	လှေသူကြီး	hlay-thŏŏ-jee:
—, under	လှေသား	hlay-*th*āh:
bricklayer, &c.	ပန်းရံသမား	pă*h*n:-yă*h*n-thă*h*mā*h*:
broker	ပွဲစား	pweh-zā*h*:
butcher	သားထိုးသမား	thā*h*:-htô*h*:-thă*h*mā*h*:
carpenter, joiner	လက်သမား	let-thă*h*mā*h*:
carter	လှည်းသမား	hleh:-thă*h*mā*h*:
clerk	စာရေး	tsă*h*-yay:
cook	အိုးသူကြီ	ô*h*:-thoo-jee:
cowherd	နွားကျောင်း	nwā*h*:-jowng:
dogkeeper	ခွေးထိန်း	hkway:-dayn:
doorkeeper	တံခါးစောင့်	tă*h*-gā*h*-zowṇg
engineer	စက်ဆရာ	tset-să*h*yā*h*
fisherman	တံငါ	tă*h*-gnā*h*
gardener	ဥယျာဉ်သည်	ŏŏ-yin-*th*eh
grasscutter	မြက်ရိတ်သမား	myet-yayk-thă*h*mā*h*:
goldsmith	ရွှေပန်းထိမ်	shway-pă*h*-dayn
groom	မြင်းထိန်း	myin:-dayn:
hunter	မုဆိုး	mo*h*k-sô*h*:
husbandman	လယ်လုပ်သမား	leh-lo*h*k-thă*h*mā*h*:
interpreter	စကားပြန်	tsă*h*-gă*h*-byă*h*n
jailor	ထောင်မှူး	htowng-hmoo:
musician	တီးမှုတ်သမား	tee:-hmo*h*k-thă*h*mā*h*:
nurse	အကလေးထိန်း	ă*h*-kă*h*-lay:-dayn:
pleader	ရှေ့နေ	shạy-nay
policeman	အမှုထမ်း။ ပုလစ်သား	ă*h*-hmŏŏ-da*h*n:, pŏŏlit-thā*h*:
potter	အိုးထိန်း	ô*h*:-dayn:
printer	ပုံနှိပ်သမား	po*h*n-hnayk-thă*h*mā*h*:

English.	Burmese.	Pronunciation.
servant	အစေအပါ။ အခစား	ăh-tsay-ăh-pāh, ăh-hkăh-zāh:
shoemaker	ဖိနပ်ချုပ်သမား	hpăh-năht-chohk-thăh-
shopkeeper	ဆိုင်သည်	sing-*th*eh [māh:
smith	ပန်းပဲ	păh-beh
tailor	အချုပ်သမား	ăh-chohk-thăhmāh:
teacher	ဆရာ။ ကျောင်းဆရာ	săhyāh, kyowng:-săh-
washerman	ခဝါသည်	hkăh-wāh-*th*eh [yāh
wet-nurse	နို့ထိန်း	nŏh-dayn:

Musical Instruments. တီးမှုတ်ရာ။

big drums	ပတ်မ။ စည်	păht-măh, tsĕĕ
clarionet	နှဲ	hneh
flute	ပုလွေ	păh-lway
gong (big)	မောင်း	mowng:
guitar (a sort of)	မိကျောင်း	mĕĕ-jowng:
harmonicon	ပတ္တလား	păht-tăh-lāh:
harp [drums	စောင်း	tsowng:
set of graduated	စည်ဝိုင်း	tsĕĕ-win:
do. gongs	ကြေးစည်ဝိုင်း	kyay:-zĕĕ-win:
trumpet	တံပိုး။ ညှင်း	tăh-bôh:, hnyin:
violin	တယော	tăh-yaw

Travelling. စီးသင်္ဘော။ လှေအားဖြင့်ခရီးသွားခြင်း။

(For Conversations, see p. 159.)

aback .	နောက်သို့	nowk-*thoh*
abaft	ပဲ့ထိမှာ	peh-zee-hmāh
alongside, to come	ဆိုက်သည်	sik-thĕĕ
anchor	ကျောက်ဆူး	kyowk-soo:

English	Burmese.	Pronunciation.
anchor (to cast)	ကျောက်ဆူးချသည်	kyowk-soo: chă*h*-*th*ëĕ
arrive (to)	ရောက်သည်	yowk-thëë
awning	နေပူကာရွက်	nay-boo-gā*h*-yŏŏet
ballast	သင်္ဘောဝမ်းစား	thim:baw-woon:-zā*h*:
berth	အိပ်ရာ	ayk-yā*h*
bill	စားရင်း	tsă*h*:-yin:
boat	သမ်ဘန်	thă*h*m-bă*h*n
bow	ဦး	oo:
buoy	ဗေါ်ရာ	bāwyā*h*
cabin	အခန်း [ထိပ်ဆံကြိုး	ă*h*-hkă*h*n: [să*h*n-jô*h*:
cable	ကျောက်ဆူးကြိုး။	kyowk-soo:-jô*h*:,htayt-
captain	သင်္ဘောသူကြီး	thim:baw-thoo-jee:
cargo	ကုန်စလယ်	ko*h*n-ză*h*-leh
carriage (vehicle)	ရထား	yă*h*-htā*h*:
change, to (train)	ပြောင်းသည်	pyowng:-*th*ee
compass	အိမ်မြှောင်အိမ်	ayn-hmyowng-ayn
crew	သင်္ဘောသားများ	thimbaw-*th*ā*h*:-myā*h*:
deck	ကုန်းပတ်	kô*h*n:-bă*h*t
depart, to	ထွက်သွားသည်	htwet-thwā*h*:-*th*ëë
dock	သင်္ဘောကျင်း	thim:baw-jin:
embark, to	သင်္ဘောတက်သည်	thim:baw-tet-*th*ëĕ
engineer	စက်ဆရာ	tset-să*h*-yā*h*
fathom	အလံ	ă*h*-lă*h*n
flag	အလံ	ă*h*-lă*h*n
forward	ဦးမှာ	oo:-hmā*h*
gangway	လှေကားပေါက်	hlay-gā*h*:-bowk
hand-lead	ရေစမ်းခဲ	yay-ză*h*n:-geh
harbour, port	သင်္ဘောဆိပ်	thim:baw-zayt
helm, rudder	တက်မ	tet-mă*h*

English.	Burmese.	Pronunciation.
hold	သင်္ဘောဝမ်း	thim:baw-woon:
keel	ဧရာ	ay-yā*h*
label [bark)	လိပ်စာ	layk-tsā*h*
land, to (disem-	သင်္ဘောဆင်းသည်	thim:baw-sin:-*th*ĕĕ
landing-stage, pier	တန်တား	tă*h*-dā*h*:
load, to	ဝန်တင်သည်	wŏŏn-tin-*th*ĕĕ
— unload	ကုန်ချသည်	kô*h*n chă*h*-*th*ĕĕ
lascar	ခလာသီ	hkă*h*-lā*h*-*th*ee
mast	ရွက်တိုင်	yŏŏet-ting
oar	ခတ်တက်	hkă*h*t-tet
paddle	လှော်တက်	hlāw-det
paddle, to	လှော်သည်	hlāw-*th*ĕĕ
passenger	စီးပါသောသူ	tsee:-pā*h*-*th*aw-thoo
pilot	မါလိန်	mā*h*layn
prow	သင်္ဘောဦးချွန်း	thim:baw-oo:-joon:
punt-pole	တိုးဝါး	tô*h*:-wā*h*:
quay	ဆိပ်	sayt
rope	ကြိုးကြီး	kyô*h*:-jee:
rudder	တက်မ	tet-mă*h*
sail	ရွက်	yŏŏ-et
sailing-ship	ရွက်တိုက်သင်္ဘော	yŏŏet-tik-thim:baw
seaman, sailor	သင်္ဘောသား	thim:baw-*th*ā*h*:
ship	သင်္ဘော	thim:baw
start, to	ထွက်သည်	htwet-thĕĕ
steam-boat, -ship	မီးသင်္ဘော	mee:-thim:baw
steersman	တက်မကိုင်	tet-mă*h*-ging
stern	ပဲ့	peh
thwart	ကန့်	kă*h*n
tiller	ထက်မကျင်	tet-mă*h*-jin

Countries and Nations. တိုင်းပြည်နှင့်လူမျိုးများ။

NOTE.—The Burmese have some few stereotyped names for people they have known long. For new ones the name or sound is caught and adapted. For country add ပြည် pyëe, and for people လူမျိုး loo-myô*h*:.

English.	Burmese.	Pronunciation.
Africa	ကပ္ပလီကျွန်း	Ká*h*ppă*h* lee-joon:
America	အမေရိက	A*h*-may-yëé-kă*h*
Arracanese	ရခိုင်	Yă*h*-hking
Bengalee	ဘင်ဂါလီ	Bin-gā*h*-lee
Burman[1]	မြန်မာ or ဗမာ	Myă*h*n-mā*h*, or Bă*h*-mā*h*
China	တရုတ်ပြည်	Tă*h*-yo*h*k-pyëĕ
Chinese, the	တရုတ်လူမျိုး	Tá*h*-yo*h*k-loo-myô*h*:
English, the	အင်ဂလိပ်လူမျိုး	Ingă*h*-layk-loo-myô*h*:
Europe	ဥရောပ	Ŏŏ-yaw-pă*h*
France	ဖရန်စစ်	Hpă*h*-yă*h*n-zit
Germany	ဇာမနီ	Zā*h*-mă*h*-nee
Holland	ဟောလန်	Haw-lă*h*n
India	အိန္ဒိယ	Ayndëé-yă*h*
Japan	ဇပန်	Ză*h*-pă*h*n
Jew	ယဟူဒီ	Yă*h*-hoo-dee
Malay	ပသျှူး	Pă*h*-shoo:
Mussulman	ပသီ	Pă*h*-thee
Persian	ပါရသီ	Pā*h*-yă*h*-thee

[1] The word Mya*h*nmā*h* is seldom used though it is the classic name. The original tribe was Mră*h*n or Myă*h*n, which was converted by the monks into the Pali form Mră*h*nmā*h*, which by natural law became Bă*h*mā*h*. The Arracanese branch of the family retain the form Mră*h*nmā*h*.

English.	Burmese.	Pronunciation.
Portuguese	ဖရင်ဂျီ	Bă*h*-yin-jee
Shan	ရှမ်း	Shă*h*n:
Siamese	ယိုးဒယား	Yô*h*:-dă*h*-yā*h*:
Talaing	တလိုင်း။ မွန်	Tă*h*-ling:, Mŏŏn

Legal Terms. တရားနှင့်စပ်ဆိုင်ရာ။

accused, the	တရားခံ	tă*h*-yă*h*-hkă*h*n
acquittal	အပြစ်လွှတ်ခြင်း။ ချမ်းသာပေးခြင်း	ă*h*-pyit-hlŏŏt-chin:, chă*h*n:-*th*a*h*-pay:-jin:
action	တရားမှု	tă*h*-yă*h*:-hmŏŏ
agent	ကိုယ်စားလှယ်	koh-ză*h*-hleh [jo*h*k
agreement, an	သဘောတူစာချုပ်	thă*h*baw-doo-tsā*h*-
answer	အဖြေ။ ထုချေချက်	ă*h*-hpyay, htŏŏ-jay-jet
appeal, to	အယူခံသည်	ă*h*-yoo hkă*h*n-*th*ëë
arrest, to	ဖမ်းဆီးသည်	hpă*h*n:-zee:-*th*ëë
attachment	သိမ်းရုံးရန်သက်မှတ်စာ	thayn:-yo*h*n:-yă*h*n-let-hmă*h*t-tsā*h*
attest, to	သက်သေခံသည်	thet-thay hkă*h*n-*th*ëë
authorize, to	အခွင့်ပေးသည်	ă*h*-hkwin pay:-*th*ëë
award, to	စီရင်ဖြတ်သည်	tsee-yin-hpyă*h*t-theé
bail	အာမခံပေးခြင်း	ā*h*mă*h*-gă*h*n pay:-jin:
bailiff	နာဇီ။ဘီလစ်	nā*h*zee, bëëlit
bond (for loan)	ငွေချေးစာချုပ်	gnway - chyay: - tsā*h* -
case (suit)	အမှု	ă*h*-hmŏŏ [jo*h*k
charge, to	စွပ်စွဲသည်	tsŏŏt-tsweh-*th*ëë
complainant, the	စွပ်စွဲသူ	tsŏŏt-tsweh-*th*oo
contract, deed	စာချုပ်	tsā*h*-jo*h*k
conviction, a	အပြစ်ပေးခြင်း	ă*h*-pyit pay:-jin:
costs	တရားစရိတ်	tă*h*-yā*h*:-ză*h*-yayt

English.	Burmese.	Pronunciation.
court (civil)	တရားမရုံး	tă*h*-yă*h*-mă*h*-yo*h*n:
court (criminal)	ရာဇဝတ်ရုံး	yā*h*-ză*h*-wŏŏt-yo*h*n:
damages	လျော်ငွေ	yāw-gnway
decision (of case)	စီရင်ချက်	tsee-yin-jet
decree	ဒီဂရီစီရင်ချက်	deegă*h*ree-tsee-yin-jet
defend, to	ကွယ်ကာစောင့်ရှောက်သည်	kweh-gā*h*-tsowng-showk-theĕ
defendant (in a suit)	တရားခံ	tă*h*-yă*h*-hkă*h*n
deposition	အစစ်ခံချက်	ă*h*-tsit-hkă*h*n-jet
document	စာတန်း၊ လိက်ခွဲတစာ	tsă*h*-dă*h*n:, layk-hkĕĕ-tă*h*-zā*h*
evidence	သက်သေထွက်ချက်	thet-thay-htwet-chet
execute, to (a deed)	လက်မှတ်ထိုးသည်	let-hmă*h*t-h ô*h*:-*th*eé
— (a judgment)	သိမ်းပိုင်ပေးသည်	thayn:-bing-pay:-*th*ĕĕ
fee (of office)	ကွမ်းဘိုး	koon:-bô*h*:
fine (penalty)	လျော်ဒါဏ်	yāw-dā*h*n
fraud	လိမ်လည်မှု	layn-lée-hmŏŏ
grant	အပိုင်ပေးစာချုပ်	ă*h*-ping-bay:-tsā*h*-jo*h*k
guardian	ထိန်းသိမ်းသူ	htayn:-thayn:-*th*oo
heir	အမွေခံ	a*h*-mway-gá*h*n
illegally	မတရားသဖြင့်	mă*h*-tă*h*-yā*h*:-*th*ă*h*-hpyin
information, to give	တိုင်ပြောသည်	ting-pyaw-*th*ée
informer	တိုင်တန်းသောသူ	ting-dă*h*n:-*th*aw-*t*oo
inheritance	အမွေဥစ္စာ	ă*h*-mway-o*h*ktsā*h*
interest	အတိုး	ă*h*-tô*h*:
inventory	ဥစ္စာပစ္စည်းစာရင်း	o*h*ktsā*h*-pyitsee:-tsá*h*-yin:
jail	ထောင်	htowng
judge, the	တရားသူကြီး	tă*h*-yā*h*:-thoo-jee:
jurisdiction (district)	စီရင်စု	tsee-yin-zŏŏ.

English.	Burmese.	Pronunciation
jurisdiction(power)	စီရင်ပိုင်သောအခွင့်	tsee-yin-bing-*th*aw ă*h*-hkwin
law-suit	တရားမှု	tă*h*:-yā*h*:-hmŏŏ [*th*ēē
non-suit, to	အယူမရှိဆိုသည်	ă*h*-yoo-mă*h*-shēēso*h*-
oath, to take an	ကျမ်းကိုင်သည်	kyă*h*n: king-*th*ēē
pardon, to	ချမ်းသာပေးသည်	chă*h*n:-*th*ā*h* pay:-*th*ēē
penal, to be	ဒါဏ်ခံထိုက်သည်	dā*h*n-hkă*h*n-dik-thēē
perjury	မထုပ်မမှန်သက်သေခံခြင်း	mă*h*-ho*h*k-mă*h*-hmă*h*n-thet-thay-hkă*h*n-
petitioner	လျှောက်သူ	showk-thoo [jin:
police-office	ပုလိစ်ရုံး	pŏŏlit-yô*h*n:
— officer	ပုလိစ်အမှုထမ်း	pŏŏlit-ă*h*-hmŏŏ-dă*h*n:
— station	ဌါန	htā*h*nă*h*
proof, to give	သက်သေပြသည်	thet-thay-pyă*h*-*th*ēē
prosecute, to	တရားပြုသည်	tă*h*-yā*h*:-pyŏŏ-*th*ēē
prosecutor, plain-	တရားလို	tă*h*-yă*h*-lo*h*
punishment [tiff	အပြစ်ဒါဏ်	ă*h*-pyit-dā*h*n
robbery	လုယူမှု	lŏŏ-yoo-hmŏŏ
seal, a	တံဆိပ်	tă*h*-zayt
sentence, a	စီရင်ချက်	tsee-yin-jet
sign, to	လက်မှတ်ထိုးသည်	let-hmă*h*t htô*h*:-*th*ēē
— (by mark)	ကြက်ခြေထိုးသည်	kyet-chee htô*h*:-*th*ēē
statement(written)	ရေးထားချက်	yay:-htā*h*:-jet
sue, to	တရားစွဲဆိုသည်	tă*h*-yā*h*:-tsweh-so*h*-
suit	အမှု	ă*h*-hmŏŏ [*th*ee
summons(of court)	သမ္မန်စာ	thămbă*h*n-zā*h*
testator	သေတမ်းစာထားသူ	thay-dă*h*n:-zā*h*-htā*h*:-
theft	ခိုးမှု	hkô*h*:-hmŏŏ [*th*oo
thief	သူခိုး	thă*h*-hkô*h*:

English.	Burmese.	Pronunciation.
trial	စစ်ကြောခြင်း	tsit-kyaw-jin:
verdict	ဆုံးဖြတ်ချက်	sô*h*n:-hpyă*h*t-chet
will	သေတန်းစာ	thay-dă*h*n:-zā*h*
witness	သက်သေ	thet-thay

Commercial Terms. ကုန်သွယ်ရာနှင့်စပ်ဆိုင်သောစကား။

English.	Burmese.	Pronunciation.
account	ငွေစာရင်း	gnway-tsā*h*-yin:
—, money	ငွေ	gnway
—, to settle an	ဖြေဆပ်သည်	hpyay-să*h*t-*th*ĕĕ
acknowledgment	ဝန်ခံချက်	wŏŏn-hkă*h*n-jet
agent	ကိုယ်စားလှယ်	ko*h*-ză*h*-hleh
arrears	ကျန်ငွေ	kyă*h*n-gnway
assets	ကြွေးဆပ်ရန်ဥစ္စာ	kyŏŏay:-să*h*t-yă*h*n-
bank	ဘန်တိုက်	bă*h*n-tik [o*h*ktsā*h*
bankrupt, to be	ကြွေးမြီကိုမဆပ်နိုင်သည်	kyŏŏay:-myee-go*h* mă*h*-să*h*t-hning-*th*ĕĕ
bearer	လက်ရှိသူ	let-shĕĕ-*th*oo
bond, a	စာချုပ်	tsā*h*-jo*h*k
broker	ပွဲစား	pweh-zā*h*:
brokerage	ပွဲခ	pweh-gă*h*
buyer	ဝယ်သူ	weh-*th*oo [ză*h*-leh
cargo	ဝန်စလယ်။ကုန်စလယ်	wŏŏn-zá*h*-leh, ko*h*n-
charter a ship, to	သင်္ဘောစာချုပ်နှင့်ငှါးသည်	thim:baw tsā*h*-jo*h*k-hnjn-hgnā*h*:-*th*ee
company	ကုမ္ပဏီ။ ကုန်ဖက်စု	kŏ*h*mbă*h*nëĕ, ko*h*n-bet-tsŏŏ
confiscate, to	သိမ်းယူသည်	thayn:-yoo-*th*ĕĕ
contract, a	ဂတိစာချုပ်	gă*h*dĕĕ-zā*h*-jo*h*k
cost price	အသိုး	ă*h*-hpô*h*:

English.	Burmese.	Pronunciation.
creditor	ကြွေးရှင်	kyŏŏay:-shin
custom-house	အကောက်တိုက်	ă*h*-kowk-tik
customs duties	အကောက်	ă*h*-kowk
damage	အကျိုးပျက်ခြင်း	ă*h*-kyô*h*:-pyet-chin:
debt	ကြွေး၊ မြီ	kyŏŏay:, myee
debtor	မြီစား	myee-zā*h*:
deliver, to	အပ်ပေးသည်	ă*h*t-pay:-*th*ĕë
exports	ထုတ်ကုန်	hto*h*k-kŏ*h*n
firm, a	ကုန်ဖက်စု	ko*h*n-bet-tsŏŏ
imports [of	သွင်းကုန်	thwin:-go*h*n
introduction, letter	အကျွမ်းဖွဲ့ပေးစာ	ă*h*-kyoon:-hpweḫ [pay:-zā*h*
market	ဈေး	zay:
market price	ဈေးနှုန်း	zay:-hnô*h*n:
partner	ဖက်စပ်သူ	hpet-tsă*h*t-thoo
pay, to	ပေးဆပ်သည်	pay:-să*h*t-thĕë
price	အဖိုး	ă*h*-hpô*h*:
price-list	အဖိုးစာရင်း	ă*h*-hpô*h*:-tsā*h*-yin:
receipt	ပြေစာ	pyay-zā*h*
rent	ငှါးခ	hgnā*h*:-gă*h*
retail, to	လက်လီရောင်းသည်	let-lee-yowng:-*th*ĕë
salesman, seller	ရောင်းသူ	yowng:-*th*oo
unload, to	ဝန်ချသည်	wŏŏn-chă*h*-*th*ĕë
warehouse	ဂိုဒေါင်၊ ကုန်လှောင် [တိုက်	go*h*downg, ko*h*n- [hlowng-dik
weight	အချိန်	ă*h*-chayn
wharf	ဆိပ်	sayt
wharfage	ဆိပ်ခ	sayt-hkă*h* [*th*ĕë
wholesale, to sell	ဖေါက်ချရောင်းသည် *or* လက်ကားရောင်းသည်	hpowk-chă*h*-yowng:-let-kā*h*:yowng:-*th*ĕë

Correspondence. မှာစာမေတ္တာစာရေးသည်နှင့်ဆိုင်ရာ။

English.	Burmese.	Pronunciation.
address	မှာစာလိပ်	hmā*h*-zā*h*-layk
blotting-paper	မှင်နှိပ်စက္ကူ	hmin-hnayk-tsekkoo
date	နေ့စွဲ	nay-zweh
dead letter office	စာသေတိုက်	tsā*h*-*th*ay-dik
envelope	စာအိတ်	tsā*h*-ayk
fasten, to	ခတ်သည်	hkă*h*t-thëë
immediate	အလျင်အမြန်	ă*h*-lyin-ă*h*-myă*h*n
ink	မှင်ရည်	hmin-yëë
inkstand	မှင်အိုး	hmin-ô*h*:
letter, note	မှာစာ။ မေတ္တာစာ	hmā*h*-zā*h*, myittā*h*-zā*h*
letter-box	ဒက်သစ်တာ	det-thittā*h*
note-paper	စာရေးစက္ကူ	tsā*h*-yay: tsekkoo
packet	အထုပ်	ă*h*-hto*h*k
pen	ကလောင်။ မှင်တံ	kă*h*lowng, hmin-dă*h*n
penknife	ဓားကလေး	dā*h*:-gá*h*lay:
pencil	ခဲတံ	hkeh-dă*h*n
post-office	ဒက်ရုံး။ စာတိုက်	det-yô*h*n:, tsā*h*-dik
quire	အလွှာ၂၄ချပ်	ă*h*-hlwā*h* hnă*h*-seh-lay:-já*h*t
ream	အလွှာ၄၀၀	ă*h*-hlwā*h*lay:-yā*h*
seal, a	တံဆိပ်	tă*h*-zayt
—, to	တံဆိပ်ခတ်သည်	tă*h*-zayt hkă*h*t-thëë
sealing-wax	ချိတ်။ သင်္ဘောချိတ်	chayt, thim:baw-jayt
sheet	အလွှာ	ă*h*-hlwā*h*
signature	လက်မှတ်	let-hmă*h*t
telegraph, to	ကြေးနန်းရိုက်သည်	kyay:-nă*h*n: yik-thëë
urgent	လျင်မြန်စွာ	lyin-myă*h*n-zŏŏā*h*
writing-materials	စာရေးရန်အရာ	tsā*h*-yay:-yă*h*n ă*h*-yā*h*

Military Terms. စစ်မှုနှင့်ဆိုင်ရာ။

English.	Burmese.	Pronunciation.
accoutrements	စစ်တန်ဆာ	tsit-tä*h*-zā*h*
ammunition	ခဲယမ်း	hkeh-yă*h*n
anvil	ပေ	pay
arms	လက်နက်	let-net *or* len-net
arsenal	လက်နက်တိုက်	let-net-tik
artillery	အမြောက်စု	ă*h*-myowk-tsŏŏ
attack, to	တိုက်သည်	tik-thëe
battery (fort)	မြေကတုတ်	myay-gă*h*-do*h*k
bayonet	သေနတ်စွပ်လှံ	thay-nă*h*t-tsŏŏt-hlă*h*n
bomb	ဗုံး	bô*h*n:
— shell	ဗုံးဆန်	bô*h*n:-ză*h*n
breach of gun	အမြောက်ရင်း	ă*h*-myowk-yin:
brigade	သူရဲတစ်စု	thoo-yeh-dă*h*t-tsŏŏ
bullet	ကျည်စေ့	kyëe-zee
camp	စားခန်း	tsä*h*-hka*h*n:
cannon	အမြောက်	ă*h*-myowk
— ball	အမြောက်ဆန်	ă*h*-myowk-să*h*n
captain	တရာဗိုလ်	tă*h*-yā*h*-bo*h*
cartridge	ယမ်းတောင့်	yă*h*n:-downg
cavalry	မြင်းစီးတပ်	myin:-zee:-tă*h*t
colonel	တထောင်ဗိုလ်	tă*h*-htowng-bo*h*
division	သူရဲတစ်စုကြီး	thŏŏ-yeh-dă*h*t-tsŏŏ-jee:
drum	စည်	tsëe
drummer	စည်တီးသမား	tsëe-tee:-thă*h*mā*h*:
fascines	ထင်းစည်း	htin:-zee:
fight, to	စစ်တိုက်သည်	tsit-tik-thëe
fosse	ကျုံး	kyô*h*n:

English.	Burmese.	Pronunciation.
furlough (leave)	အခွင့်	ă*h*-hkwịn
general	ဗိုလ်ချုပ်	bo*h*-jo*h*k
guard (house)	ကင်းတဲ	kin:-deh
guide	လမ်းပြ	lă*h*n:-byă*h*
haversack	လွယ်အိတ်	lweh-ayk
hospital	လူနာရုံ	loo-nā*h*-yo*h*n
helmet	ခမောက်	hkă*h*-mowk
infantry	ခြေသည်	chyay-theh
lock of gun	သေနတ်မီးအိမ်	thay-nă*h*t mee:-ayn
magazine	ယမ်းတိုက်	yă*h*n:-dik
major	ငါးရာဗိုလ်	gnā*h*:-yāh-bo*h*
mallet	လက်ရိုက်	let-yik
mine	မြေတွင်း	myay-dwin:
mutiny	ပုန်ကန်ခြင်း	po*h*n-kă*h*n-jin:
officer	ဗိုလ်။ စစ်ဗိုလ်	bo*h*, tsit-bo*h*
outpost	ကင်းတပ်	kin:-dă*h*t
picket (peg)	သစ်ချွန်။ စို့	thit-chōōn, tsọ*h*
platform	စင်	tsin
powder	ယမ်းတပ်	yă*h*n:
rammer	ထိုးတံ	htô*h*:-dă*h*n
regiment	တပ်	tă*h*t
rifle, gun	ရိုက်ပတ်။ သေနတ်	yik-pă*h*t, thay-nă*h*t
— barrel	ရိုက်ပတ်ပြောင်း	yik-pă*h*t-pyowng:
— cock	မောင်း	mowng:
— stock	ရိုက်ပတ်အိမ်	yik-pă*h*t-ayn
sentry	အစောင့်	ă*h*-tsowṇg
soldiers	စစ်သည်။ တပ်သား	tsit-thee, tă*h*t-thā*h*:
— (European)	ဂေါရာ	gāw-yā*h*
sword	ဓားလွယ်	dă*h*-lweh

English.	Burmese.	Pronunciation.
shovel	တူးရွင်းပြား	too:-yŏŏin:-byā*h*:
stockade	သစ်တပ်	thit-tă*h*t
town wall	မြို့ရိုး	myọ*h*-yô*h*:
trigger	လက်လှုပ်	let-hlo*h*k
war	စစ်။ စစ်တိုက်ခြင်း	tsit, tsit-tik-chin:

Religion. အယူဘာသာ။

English.	Burmese.	Pronunciation.
ascetic	ဖိုးသူတော်	hpô*h*:-thọo-dāw
begging-bowl	သပိတ်	thă*h*bayt
bell (large)	ခေါင်းလောင်း	hkowng:-lowng:
— (small)	ဆည်းလည်း	see:-lee:
books	စာအုပ်	tsā*h*-o*h*k
— sacred (Bible)	ကျမ်း။ ပိဋကတ်	kyā*h*n:, peedă*h*kă*h*t
Buddha	ဘုရားသခင်။ ဗုဒ္ဓ	hpă*h*-yā*h*: thă*h*-hken, bo*h*k-dă*h*
Buddhist religion	ဗုဒ္ဓဘာသာ	bo*h*kdă*h*-bā*h*thā*h*
cemetery	သင်းချိုင်	thin:-jin
Christian	ခရစ်ယာန်	hkă*h*-yit-yā*h*n
Christianity	ခရစ်ဘာသာ	hkă*h*-yit-bā*h*thā*h*
church (Buddhist)	သံဃာ	thinghā*h*
— (other bodies)	အသင်းတော်	ă*h*-thin:-dāw
— (building)	သုဓမ္မာဇရပ်	thŏŏdă*h*mmă*h*-ză*h*yă*h*t
clergyman	ဆရာ။ ဓမ္မဆရာ	să*h*-yā*h*, dă*h*mmā*h*-să*h*-yā*h*
coffin	တလား	tă*h*-lā*h*
congregation	ပရိသတ်	pă*h*-yayk-thă*h*t
convent (for nuns)	မယ်သူတော်ကျောင်း	meh-thoo-dāw-jowng:
corpse	အလောင်း	ă*h*-lowng:
Creator, the	ဖန်ဆင်းတော်မူသော ဘုရားသခင်	hpă*h*n-zin:-dāw-moo-*th*aw-hpă*h*-yā*h*:-thă*h*-hken

English.	Burmese.	Pronunciation.
cross	ထက်ဝါးကပ်တိုင်	let-wā*h*:-gă*h*t-ting
fast, to	အစာရှောင်သည်	ă*h*-tsā*h* showng-*th*ĕĕ
fast-day	ဥပုတ်နေ့	ŏŏbo*h*k-nay
festival	ပွဲနေ့	pweh-nay
funeral	မသာ	mă*h*-thā*h*
— of monk	ဘုံးကြီးပြံ	hpô*h*n:-jee:-byă*h*n
funeral rite, to per-	သင်ဂြိုဟ်သည်	thin-jô*h*-*th*ĕĕ
ghosts [form	တစ္ဆေ	tă*h*-say
God	ဘုရားသခင်	hpă*h*-yā*h*:-thă*h*-hken
heaven	မိုဃ်း။ ကောင်းကင်	mô*h*:, kowng:-gin
hell	ငရဲ	gnă*h*-yeh
hermit	ရသေ့	yă*h*-thay
image	ရုပ်တု	yo*h*k-tŏŏ
monastery	ကျောင်း	kyowng:
— precincts	ကျောင်းတိုက်	kyowng:-dik
monk	ရဟန်း။ ဘုန်းကြီး	yă*h*-hă*h*n:, hpô*h*n:-jee:
monk's dress	သင်္ကန်း	thingă*h*n:
nun	မယ်သူတော်	meh-thoo-dāw
pagoda	စေတီ။ ဘုရား	zay-dee, hpă*h*-yā*h*:
pray	ဆုတောင်းသည်	sŏŏ-downg:-*th*ee
probationer	မောင်ရှင်။ သာမဏေ	mowng-yin, thā*h*mă*h*-
preach, to	တရားဟောသည်	tă*h*-yā*h*: haw-*th*ĕĕ [nay
religion	သာသနာတော်	thā*h*-*th*ă*h*-nā*h*-dāw
rest-house	ဇရပ်	ză*h*-yă*h*t
scholar [ings	တပည့်	tă*h*-beh
supernatural[1] be-	နတ်။ ဒေဝ	nă*h*t, daywă*h*

[1] The '*năht*' is a supernatural being answering to the fairy or kelpie. *Dewăh* is the Pali name connected with Lat. *deus*. They are supposed to be everywhere and have to be appeased by small sacrifices. The *năgāh*: lives in the water and underground and corresponds to the *drak* or dragon.

English.	Burmese.	Pronunciation.
supernatural ser-	နဂါး	nă*h*gā*h*:
umbrella [pents	ထီး	htee:
water-tank	ရေကန်	yay-gă*h*n
weathercock	ငှက်မနား	hgnet-mă*h*-nā*h*:

Society and Government. အမိုးရမင်းနှင့်အရာရှိတို့

circle (division of a district)	တိုက်	tik
—, head man of	တိုက်သူကြီး	tik thă*h*-jee:
citizen	မြို့သား	myo*h*-*thāh*: [jee:
commissioner	ဝန်ရှင်တော်မင်းကြီး	wŏŏn-shin-dāw min:-
assistant do.	ဝန်ထောက်တော်မင်း	wŏŏn-dowk-dāw-min:
deputy do.	အရေးပိုင်မင်း	ă*h*-yay:-bing-min:
forest officer	သစ်တောဝန်ထောက်	thit-taw wŏŏn-dowk
judge	တရားမသူကြီး	tă*h*-yă*h*-mă*h* thă*h*-jee:
king	ရှင်ဘုရင်	shin-bă*h*-yin
kingdom	နိုင်ငံ	ning-gnă*h*n
landowner	မြေရှင်	myay-shin
lessee of fishery	အင်းသူကြီး	in: thă*h*-jee:
magistrate	ရာဇဝတ်မင်း	yā*h*ză*h*wŏŏt-min:
— (of town)	မြို့ဝန်	myo*h* wŏŏn
minister of state	အတွင်းဝန်	ă*h*-twin: wŏŏn
peasant	ကျေးတောသား	kyay:-daw-*thāh*:
people	ပြည်သူပြည်သား	pyee-*th*oo pyee-*thāh*:
prince, princess	မင်းသား။ မင်းသမီး	min:-*thāh*:, min:-*thăh*-
province, division	နယ်။ ခရိုင်	neh, hkă*h*-ying [mee:
queen (own right)	ဘုရင်မ	bă*h*-yin-mă*h*
— (of king)	မိဖုရား	mëë-bă*h*-yā*h*:

English.	Burmese.	Pronunciation.
revenue	အခွန်	ăh-hkŏŏn [jee:
secretary	စာရေး။ စာရေးကြီး	tsăh-yay:, tsăh-yay:
secretary (chief)	အတွင်းဝန်ထောက်	ăh-twin: wŏŏn-dowk
timber-forest-contractor [trate	သစ်ခေါင်း	thit-gowng:
township magis-	မြို့အုပ်	myọh-ohk
village constable	ရွာခေါင်း	yŏŏăh-gowng:
— elder	ရွာလူကြီး	yŏŏăh-loo-jee:
villager	ရွာသား။ (f.) ရွာသူ	yŏŏăh-*thăh*:, (f.) yŏŏăh-*thoo*

Government Departments. အဓိရရေးဌာန။

Accounts	ငွေတိုက်ရေးဌာန	Ǫnway-dik-yay: htăh-năh
Cadastral Survey	လယ်ရာရေးဌာန	Leh-yăh yay: htăhnăh
Civil	တရားမရေးဌာန	Tăhyăh-măh yay: htăhnăh
Customs	အကောက်ရေးဌာန	Ăh-kowk yay: htăhnăh
Education	ပညာရေးဌာန	Peenyăh yay: htăhnăh:
Foreign	နိုင်ငံခြားရေးဌာန	Ning-gnăhn-chăh: yay: htăhnăh
Forest	သစ်တောရေးဌာန	Thit-taw yay: htăhnăh
General	အရပ်ရပ်ရေးဌာန	Ăh-yăht-yăht yay: htăhnăh [năh
Home	နိုင်ငံရေးဌာန	Ning-gnăhn yay: htăh-
Jail	အကျဉ်းရေးဌာန	Ăh-kyin: yay: htăhnăh
Judicial	တရားရာဇဝတ်ရေးဌာန:	Tăhyăh: yăhzạh-wŏŏt yay: htăhnăh

English.	Burmese.	Pronunciation.
Legislative	ဥပဒေပြုဌာန	Ŏŏpă*h*day-pyŏŏ htā*h*-
Military	စစ်ရေးဌာန	Tsit yay: htā*h*nă*h* [nă*h*
Police	ရာဇဝတ်ရေးဌာန	Yā*h*ză*h*-wŏŏt yay: htā*h*nă*h*
Postal	စာတိုက်ရေးဌာန	Tsā*h*-dik yay: htā*h*nă*h*
Public-Works	နိုင်ငံတွတ်လုပ်ဆောင် ရေးဌာန	Ning-gnă*h*n-dwet-lo*h*k-sowng yay: htā*h*nă*h*
Revenue	အခွန်တော် ရေးဌာန	Ă*h*-hkŏŏn-dāw yay: htā*h*nă*h*
Revenue Settle- [ment	ကြေးထိုင်ဌာန	Kyay:-ding htā*h*nă*h*
Telegraph	ကြေးနန်းရေးဌာန	Kyay:-nā*h*n: yay:-htā*h*-nā*h*

Govt. Prosecutor	အစိုးရအမှုလိုက်ရှေ့ နေ	Ă*h*-tsô*h*:-yă*h* ă*h*-hmŏŏ-lik shay-nay [byă*h*n
do. Translator	အစိုးရစာတော်ပြန်	Ă*h*-tsô*h*:-yă*h* tsā*h*-dāw-
Supt. of Government Printing	အစိုးရပုံနှိတ်တိုက် အုပ်	Ă*h*-tsô*h*:-yă*h* po*h*n-hnayk-tik-o*h*k

The Cardinal Numbers. ဂဏန်းများနှင့်အမည်။

(For Grammatical Notes, see, p. 114.)

	Burmese character.	Burmese words.	Pronunciation.
1	၁	တစ်	tit (*or* tăh in composition)
2	၂	နှစ်	hnit (*or* hnăh in composi- [tion)
3	၃	သုံး	thô*h*n:
4	၄	လေး	lay:
5	၅	ငါး	gnā*h*:
6	၆	ခြောက်	chowk
7	၇	ခုနှစ်	hkŏŏ-hnit
8	၈	ရှစ်	shit
9	၉	ကိုး	kô*h*:
10	၁၀	တဆယ်	tă*h* seh
11	၁၁	တဆယ့်နှင့်တစ်	tă*h* seh hnin̥[1] tit *or* seh-tit
12	၁၂	တဆယ့်နှင့်နှစ်	tă*h* seh hnin̥ hnit
13	၁၃	တဆယ့်နှင့်သုံး	tă*h* seh hnin̥ thô*h*n:
14	၁၄	တဆယ့်နှင့်လေး	tă*h* seh hnin̥ lay:
15	၁၅	တဆယ့်နှင့်ငါး	tă*h* seh hnin̥ gnā*h*:
16	၁၆	တဆယ့်နှင့်ခြောက်	tă*h* seh hnin̥ chowk
17	၁၇	တဆယ့်နှင့်ခုနှစ်	tă*h* seh hnin̥ khŏŏ-hnit
18	၁၈	တဆယ့်နှင့်ရှစ်	tă*h* seh hnin̥ shit
19	၁၉	တဆသ့်နှင့်ကိုး	tă*h* seh hnin̥ kô*h*:
20	၂၀	နှစ်ဆယ်	hnit seh *or* hnă*h* seh
21	၂၁	နှစ်ဆယ့်နှင့်တစ်	hnit seh hnin̥ tit *or* hnă*h* [seh tit
30	၃၀	သုံးဆယ်	thô*h*n: zeh
40	၄၀	လေးဆယ်	lay: zeh
50	၅၀	ငါးဆယ်	gnā*h*: zeh

[1] The နှင့် hnin̥, *and*, may always be left out.

	Burmese character.	Burmese words.	Pronunciation.
60	၆၀	ခြောက်ဆယ်	chowk seh
70	၇၀	ခုနှစ်ဆယ်	hkŏŏ-hnit seh
80	၈၀	ရှစ်ဆယ်	shit seh
90	၉၀	ကိုးဆယ်	kô*h*: zeh
100	၁၀၀	တရာ	tă*h* yā*h*
101	၁၀၁	တရာနှင့်တစ်	tă*h* yā*h* hnin̥ tit
110	၁၁၀	တရာတဆယ်	tă*h* yā*h* tă*h* seh
200	၂၀၀	နှစ်ရာ	hnă*h* yā*h*
1,000	၁၀၀၀	တထောင်း	tă*h* htowng:
10,000	၁၀၀၀၀	တသောင်း	tă*h* thowng:
1,000,000	၁၀၀၀၀၀၀	တသန်း	tă*h* thă*h*n

A.D. 1910, ၁၉၁၀, tă*h* htowng: ko*h*: yā*h* ta*h* seh.

Numeral Auxiliaries.[1]

Burmese.	Pronunciation.	Meaning.	Use.
အဦး	ă*h*-oo:	That which is first or chief	For rational beings
အကောင်	ă*h*-kowng	An animal	For brute beasts
အကြောင်း	ă*h*-kyowng:	An extended line	For extended things, like roads
အကွင်း	ă*h*-kwin:	A ring, circle	For rings, nooses, &c.
အခု	ă*h*-hkŏŏ	(Uncertain)	For things which cannot be described
အချပ်	ă*h*-chă*h*t	A flat thing	For flat and thin things, like mats

[1] See p. 114.

Burmese.	Pronunciation.	Meaning.	Use.
အချောင်း	ă*h*-chowng:	A bar	For things long and straight, as needles
အခွန်း	ă*h*-hkŏŏn:	(Uncertain)	For words
အဝင်း	ă*h*-tsin:	From ဝင်း tsin:, to extend in a line	Things long and straight, as spears and boats
အစီး	ă*h*-tsee:	What is ridden on	As horses and carts
အစောင်	ă*h*-tsowng	(Uncertain)	Writings, books
အဆူ	ă*h*-soo	(Uncertain)	For pagodas
အဆောင်	ă*h*-sowng	A building	For houses, roofs
အတန်	ă*h*-tă*h*n	An interval	Things occurring at intervals of space or time
အထည်	ă*h*-hteh	A piece of cloth	For clothing
အပင်	ă*h*-pin	A plant	For plants
အပါး	ă*h*-pā*h*:	Meaning is uncertain, but probably from ပါး pā*h*:, *to be separate*	For deities, ecclesiastics, and persons in power
အပြား	ă*h*-pyā*h*:	Flat things	As boards
အဖက်	ă*h*-hpet	A side	For things usually in pairs, as hands
အလက်	ă*h*-let	A hand	Weapons, tools, or what is used in the hand
အလုံး	ă*h*-lô*h*n:	What is round	Things round or [cubical
အသွယ်	ă*h*-thweh	What is slender	As rivers
ယောက်	yowk	An old root, meaning uncertain, but used in connection with men.	For ordinary men and women

Examples.

English.	Burmese.	Pronunciation.
Three men	လူသုံးယောက်	Loo thô*h*n: yowk
Five trees	သစ်ပင်ငါးပင်	Thit-pin gnā*h*: bin
Six dogs	ခွေးခြောက်ကောင်	Hkway: chowk kowng
Four rupees	ဒင်္ဂါလေးပြား	Dingā*h* lay: byā*h*.
Two objects of worship	ဘုရားနှစ်ဆူ	Hpă*h*yā*h*: hnit soo
One cart	လှည်းတစီး	Hleh: tă*h* zee:
Four canoes	လှေလေးစင်း	Hlay lay: zin:
A table	စားပွဲတခု	Tsă*h*-bweh tă*h* hkŏŏ
Three monks	ရဟန်းသုံးပါး	Yá*h*ä*h*n: thô*h*n: bā*h*:
Two fingers	လက်ချောင်းနှစ်ချောင်း	Let-chowng: hnă*h* chowng:
A word	စကားတခွန်း	Tsa*h*gā*h*: tă*h* hkŏŏn:

Ordinal Numerals. အစီအစဉ်ကိုပြသောသင်္ချာဂဏန်း

(For Grammatical Notes, see p. 115.)

first	ပဌမ	pă*h*-hṭă*h*-mă*h*
second	ဒုတိယ	dŏŏ-tëë-yă*h*
third	တတိယ	tă*h*-tëë-yă*h*
fourth	စတုတ္ထ	tsă*h*-do*h*k-htă*h*
fifth	ပဉ္စမ	pyin-tsă*h*-mă*h*
sixth	ဆဋ္ဌမ	să*h*-hṭă*h*-mă*h*
seventh	သတ္တမ	thă*h*t-tă*h*-mă*h*
eighth	အဋ္ဌမ	ă*h*-hṭă*h*-mă*h*
ninth	နဝမ	nă*h*-wă*h*-mă*h*
tenth	ဒသမ	dă*h*-thă*h*-mă*h*

English.	Burmese.	Pronunciation.
eleventh	ဧကဒသမ	ay-kah-dăh-thăh-măh
twelfth	ဒွါဒသမ	dwāh-dăh-thăh-măh

The above are all Pali words, and are not used beyond twelve. Being polysyllables they ought not to be divided, but the hyphen is used to assist pronunciation.

Collective and Fractional Numbers.

အရေအတွက်တွင်ပိုင်းချားရပုံသောစကားများ

all	အားလုံး။ ခပ်သိမ်း	āh:-lôhn:, hkăht-thayn:
couple, a	နှစ်ခု။ တရံ။ တစုံ	hnăh-hkŏŏ, tăh-yăhn, [tah-zŏhn
double	နှစ်ဆ	hnăh-săh
dozen, a	ဆယ်နှစ်ခု	seh-hnăh-hkŏŏ
fifth, a	ငါးပိုင်းတပိုင်း	gnāh:-bing: tăh-bing:
firstly	အဦးဆုံး	áh-oo:-zôhn:
once	တခါ။ တချိန်။ တပန်။ တလီ	tăh-hkāh, tăh-jayn, tăh-hpăhn, tăh-lee
one-half	တဝက်	tăh-wet
exactly half	ထက်ဝက်	htet-wet
pair, a	အစုံ။ အရံ	ăh-tsohn, ăh-yăhn
part, portion	အပိုင်း	ăh-ping:
quarter, fourth	တစိတ်	tăh-zayt
single [part	တခုထည်း	tăh-gŏŏ-dee: [1]
third, a	သုံးပိုင်းတပိုင်း	thôhn: bing:tăh-bing:
threefold	သုံးဆ	thôhn:-zăh

[1] Where ခု is not used above as the numerical affix, it will be necessary to use the proper affix given at pp. 79-81 instead

Also instead of ပိုင်း ping *a portion*, one may use ပုံ pöhn, *heap*, or စု tsŏŏ, *collection*.

English.	Burmese.	Pronunciation.
three-quarters	သုံးစိတ်	thôhn:-zayt
three-sevenths	ခုနစ်ပုံသုံးပုံ	hköö-hnăh-bohn-thôhn:-bohn
twice	နှစ်ခါ	hnăh-hkāh [hnăh-zöö
two-sixths	ခြောက်ခုမှာနှစ်ခု	chowk-tsöö-hmāh
whole, the	အကုန်။ အလုံး	ăh-kôhn, ăh-lôhn:

Adjectives (*Intransitive Verb Roots*).[1] ဝိသေသနပဒ။

သော *th*aw must be added to each if used in front of a noun.

(For Grammatical Notes, see p. 113.)

able (capable)	တတ်။ တတ်နိုင်။ တတ်စွမ်း	tăht, tăht-hning, tăht-tsoon:
awake	နိုးနေ။ နိုး	nôh:-nay, nôh:
bad (wicked)	ဆိုး	soh:
— (unsound)	မကောင်း	măh kowng:
base	ယုတ်	yohk
beautiful, hand-	လှ	hlăh
beloved [some	ချစ်	chit
big	ကြီး	kyee:
bitter	ခါး	hkāh:
blind	ကန်း	kăhn:

[1] Adjectives are often used in pairs to prevent mistake. Thus,—

နက် net means *deep, not shallow*; it also means *to be dark*.

နက်နဲ net-neh means *intellectually deep, profound*.

လှ hlăh, *handsome* and also *very*. So to prevent mistake we may say လှပ hlăhbăh, *handsome*. ပ păh by itself means *shiny*.

English.	Burmese.	Pronunciation.
blunt	တုံး	tô*h*n:
bold, brave	ရဲ။ ရဲရင့်	yeh, yeh-yiṇ
bright	ပြောင်	pyowng
broad, wide	ကျယ်	kyeh
careful	သတိပြုတတ်	thă*h*dĕĕ pyŏŏ-dă*h*t
careless	သတိလစ်	thă*h*dĕĕ lit
cheap	အဖိုးချို	ă*h*-hpô*h*: cho*h*
clean	စင်။ စင်ကြယ်။ သန့်	tsin, tsin-kyeh, thă*h*ṇ-
clear	ကြည်လင် [ရှင်း	kyee-lin [shin:
clever	လိမ္မာ	laymmā*h*
cold	ချမ်း	chă*h*n:
comfortable	သက်သာ	thet-thā*h*
cool	ဧ။ အေး	ay:
corpulent	ဝ။ ဖျိုး	wă*h*, hpyôh:
costly	အဖိုးကြီး	ă*h*-hpô*h*: kyee:
crazy	ရူး။ သွတ်။ စိတ်ရူး	yoo:, thŏŏt, tsayt-yoo:
cruel	ရက်စက် [ပေါက်	yet-tset [powk
damp	ထိုင်း	hting:
dark	မှောင်။ မိုက်။ ညို	hmowng, mik, nyo*h*
deaf	နားပင်း။ နားလေး	nā*h*: pin:, nā*h*: lay:
dear (in price)	အဖိုးကြီး	ă*h*-hpô*h*: kyee:
deep (not shallow)	နက်	net
— (of purpose)	နက်နဲ	net-neh
different	ခြားနား။ ကွဲပြား။ ထူး	chā*h*:-nā*h*:, kweh-
dim	မှုန်	hmŏ*h*n [byāh:, htoo:
dirty	ညစ်	nyit
dry	သွေ့။ ခြောက်	thwạy, chowk
dull (of weather)	အုံ့	o*h*ṇ
dumb	အ	ă*h*

English.	Burmese.	Pronunciation.
dusty	ဖုံထ။ ဖုံထူ	hpo*h*n-htă*h*, hpo*h*n-htoo
early	စော	tsaw
easy (to do)	လွယ်	lweh
empty	လွတ်လပ်	lŏŏt-lă*h*t
even	ညီညာ	nyee-nyā*h*
false	မဟုတ်။ မမှန်	mă*h*-ho*h*k, mă*h*-hmă*h*n
far	ဝေး	way:
few	နည်း။ ရှား	neh:, shā*h*:
fine (excellent)	ကောင်းမြတ်။ မြတ်	kowng:-myă*h*t, myă*h*t
— (in quality)	ချော။ ညက်	chaw, nyet
fit (for)	တော်လျော်	tāw-lyāw
flat	ပြား။ ပြန့်	pyā*h*:, pyă*h*n̥
foolish	မိုက်။ နှမ်း	mik, hnă*h*n:
fortunate	ကံကောင်း	kă*h*n-gowng:
free	ကင်းလွတ်	kin:-lŏŏt
fresh	လန်း။ သစ်	lă*h*n:, thit
full	ပြည့်စုံ	pyē̥-zo*h*n
gay	ရွှင်လန်း။ ဝမ်းမြောက်	shwin-lă*h*n:, woon: myowk
general, usual	ဖြစ်လေ့	hpyit-lḁy
gentle	နူးညံ့	noo:-nyăhn̥
glad	ရွှင်လန်း	shwin-lă*h*n:
good	ကောင်း	kowng:
grand	မြင့်မြတ်	myin̥-myă*h*t
great	ကြီး။ (P.) မဟာ	kyee:, (P.) mă*h*hā*h*
happy	ချမ်းသာ	chă*h*n:-*thă*h*
hard	မာ	mā*h*
— (difficult)	ခက်ခဲ	hket-hkeh
— (disposition)	ကြမ်းထမ်း	kyă*h*n:-dă*h*n:
heavy	လေး	lay:

English.	Burmese.	Pronunciation.
high	မြင့်	myin̥
honest	ဖြောင့်မတ်။ ရိုးသား	hpyown̥g-mă*h*t, yô*h*:-[thă*h*:
hot	ပူ	poo
hungry	မွတ်သိတ်	mŏŏt-thayt
ill (unwell)	နာ။ မမာ	nā*h*, mă*h*-mā*h*
important	ဂရုပြုဘွယ်	gă*h*yŏŏ pyŏŏ-bweh
just	ဖြောင့်မတ်	hpyown̥g-mă*h*t
lame	ခြေမစွမ်း	chyay mă*h* tsoon:
large, vast	ကြီးကျယ်	kyee:-kyeh
last	နောက်ဆုံး	nowk-sô*h*n:
late	နောက်ကျ	nowk-kyă*h*
lazy	ပျင်း။ ပျင်းရိ	pyin:, pyin:-yĕĕ
lean	ပိန်။ကြုံ	payn, kyo*h*n
light (not heavy)	ပေါ့	paw
light (not dark)	လင်း	lin:
like	တူ	too
little (small)	ငယ်။ ကလေး	gneh:, kă*h*lay:
long	ရှည်	shay
— (of time)	ကြာ	kyā*h*
loose	မကျပ်။ ချောင်	mă*h* kyă*h*t, chowng
low (in place)	နိမ့်	nayn̥
— (in spirits)	ညှိုးငယ်	hnyo*h*:-gne*h*
many	များ	myā*h*:
mild	နူးညံ့။ သိမ်မွေ့	noo: - nyăh̥n, thayn - [mwḁy
muddy	နောက်	nowk
natural	သဘာဝ။ နဂိုရ်	thă*h*bā*h*wă*h*, nă*h*go*h*
near	နီး။ နား	nee:, nā*h*:
new	သစ်	thit
nice, tasty	ဆိမ့်။ အရသာရှိ	sayn̥, ă*h*-yă*h*-*thăh* shĕĕ

English.	Burmese.	Pronunciation.
old[1] (not new)	ဟောင်း	howng:
open	ပွင့်	pwiṉ
— (gaping)	ဟ	hä*h*
patient	သည်းခံ	thee:-hkä*h*n
pleasant	သာ။ သာယာ	thā*h*, thā*h*-yā*h*
poor (not rich)	ဆင်းရဲ	sin:-yeh
poor (in quality)	ညံ့	nyä*h*ṉ
poor (to be pitied)	သနားဘွယ်	thă*h*nā*h*:-bweh
possible	ဖြစ်နိုင်	hpyit-ning
pretty	လှ။ တင့်တယ်	hlä*h*, tiṉ-deh
private (secluded)	ဆိတ်ကွယ်	sayt-kweh
— (personal)	ကိုယ်နှင့်သာဆိုင်	ko*h*-hniṉ *thāh* sing
probable	ဖြစ်လးတ္တံ့။ ဖြစ်ကောင်း	hpyit-lă*h*ttă*h*ṉ, hpyit-kowng:
proud	စိတ်မြင့်။ ထောင်မောင်	tsayt-myiṉ, htāw-māw
pure, clean	စင်ကြယ်။ သန့်ရှင်း	tsin-kyeh, thä*h*ṉ-shin:
quick, swift	လျင်။ မြန်	lyin, myă*h*n
quiet	ငြိမ်သက်	gnyayn-thet
— (scarce)	ရှားပါး	shā*h*:-bā*h*:
raw	စိမ်း	tsayn:
rich	ကြွယ်ဝ	kyŏŏ-eh-wă*h*
right, true	မှန်။ ဟုတ်	hmă*h*n, ho*h*k
ripe	မှည့်	hmeh̥
rough	ကြမ်း	kyă*h*n:
round	လုံး	lô*h*n:
rude	ရိုင်း။ ရိုင်းပြ	ying, ying:-byă*h*
sad	စိတ်ပူ။ ဝမ်းနည်း	tsayt-poo, wŏŏn: neh:

[1] Old (in age) အို။ အသက်ကြီး. ဟောင်း is used only for inanimate things, except in the sense of *former*, like French *ancien*.

English.	Burmese.	Pronunciation.
safe, secure	လုံချုံ	lo*h*n-cho*h*n
sharp	ထက်	htet
— (of sound)	စူး	tsoo:
short	တို	to*h*
— (of time)	မကြာ	mă*h* kyā*h*
short (in stature)	ပု	pŏŏ
silent	တိတ်ဆိတ်	tayt-sayt
slow	နှေး။ ဖြည်းညှင်း	hnay:, hpyay:-hnyin:
small	ငယ်။ သေး	gneh, thay:
smooth	ချော။ ပြေပြစ်	chaw, pyay-byit
soft	ပျော့။ နူးညံ့	pyaw, noo:-nyă*h*n̥
sour	ချဉ်	chin
square	စတုရန်းဖြစ်	tsă*h*dŏŏyă*h*n: hpyit
straight	ဖြောင့်	hpyowng̥
strange (curious)	ထူးဆန်း	htoo:-ză*h*n:
strong	စွမ်းမာ။ အားကြီး	tsŏŏn:-mă*h*, ā*h*:-kyee:
stupid, dull	ညာဏ်ထုံ။ ထိုင်းမှိုင်း	nyā*h*n - htô*h*n, hting:-hming:
sufficient	လောက်	lowk
sweet	ချို	cho*h*
— smelling	မွှေး	hmway:
tall	အရပ် မြင့်	ă*h*-yă*h*t-myin̥
thick (stout)	ထုတ်	to*h*k
—, dense	ပျစ်	pyit
thin	ပါး။ မပျစ်	pā*h*:, mă*h* pyit
thirsty	ရေငတ်	yay-gnă*h*t
tough	ပျဉ်း။ ခိုင်ခံ့	pyin:, hking-gă*h*n̥
ugly	အရုပ်ဆိုး။ မလှ	ă*h*-yo*h*k sô*h*:, mă*h* hlă*h*
useful	အသုံးဝင်။ အကျိုးရှိ	ă*h*-thô*h*n: win, ă*h*-kyô*h*: shëe
usual	ဖြစ်လေ့ရှိ	hpyit-lay̥ shëe

English.	Burmese.	Pronunciation.
valuable	အဘိုးထိုက်။ အဘိုးတန်	ăh-hpôh: htik, ăh-hpôh: tăhn
various	ထူးခြား။ အထူးထူး	htoo:-jāh:, ăh-htoo:doo:
warm	နွေး။ အိုက်	nway:, ik
weak	အားနည်း။ ချိနဲ့။ ပေါ့	āh:neh:, cheh-neh, paw
wet	စို။ စိုစွတ်	tsoh, tsoh-zŏŏt
willing	စိတ်ပါ	tsayt-pāh
wise	ပညာရှိ	pyinyāh shēē
wrong	မမှန်	măh hmăhn
— (erroneous)	မှားလွဲ	hmāh:-lweh
young	အသက်ငယ်	ăh-thet gneh

Verbs. ကြိယာ။

(For Grammatical Notes, see p. 115.)

[Most of the Intransitive Verbs will be found with the adjectives. သည် *thēē* to be added to each.]

To accept (agree)	ဝန်ခံ	wŏŏn-hkăhn
„ — (receive)	ခံယူ	hkăhn-yoo
„ ache	ကိုက်	kik
„ acquire	ရ။ ရမိ	yăh, yăh-mēē
„ add	ပေါင်း	powng:
„ admire	နှစ်သက်	hnit-thet
„ admonish	ဆုမ္မ	sôhmmăh
„ adore (trust in)	ကိုးကွယ်	kôh:-gweh
„ advance	တိုးတက်	tôh:-tet
„ aid	ကူညီ	koo-nyee
„ answer, reply	ထုချေ။ ပြန်ပြော	htŏŏ-jyay, pyăhn-pyaw
„ applaud	ချီးမွမ်း	chee:-moon:

English.	Burmese.	Pronunciation.
To appoint	ခန့်ထား	hkăhṇ-htāh:
„ approve	စိတ်တူ	tsayt-too
„ arise	ထ။ *intr.* ထစေ။ *tr.*	htăh, htăh-zay
„ arrange	ပြင်ဆင်	pyin-zin
„ arrive	ရောက်။ ဆိုက်	yowk, sik
„ ascend	တက်	tet
„ ask	မေး	may:
„ — (demand)	တောင်း	towng:
„ assemble	စုဝေး။ *tr.* or *intr.*	tsŏŏ-way:
„ avoid	ရှောင်	showng
„ awaken	နိုး။ နိုးဆော်	hnôh:, hnôh:-zāw
„ bathe	ရေချိုး။ *intr.*	yay chôh:
„ be	ဖြစ်။ ရှိ	hpyit, shee
„ beat	ရိုက်။ ပုတ်။ နှက်	yik, pohk, hnet
„ begin	အစပြု	ăh-tsăh pyŏŏ
„ believe	ယုံ [ကွေး။ *intr.*	yohn
„ bend	ညွတ်။ *tr.* ညွှတ်။	hnyŏŏt, nyŏŏt, kwạy
„ bind	ချည်။ ချည်နှောင်	chĕĕ, chĕe-hnowng
„ bite	ကိုက်	kik
„ blame	အပြစ်တင်	ăh-pyit tin
„ blow	မှုတ်	hmohk
„ — (as wind)	တိုက်	tik
„ boast	ဝါကြွား	wāh-kyŏŏāh:
„ boil	ပြုတ်။ ချက်	pyŏhk, chet
„ borrow	ချေးငှါး [ဖဲ့။ *tr.*	chee:-hgnāh: [hpẹh
„ break	ကျိုး။ *intr.* ခွဲ။ ဖြို။	kyôh:, hkweh, hpyoh,
„ bring	ယူလာ။ ယူခဲ့။ ဆောင်	yoo-lāh, yoo-geḥ,
„ build	ဆောက် [ယူ။ *tr.*	sowk [sowng-yoo
„ burn	မီးလောင်။ *intr.*	mee: lowng

English.	Burmese.	Pronunciation.
To burn (set fire to)	မီးရှို့	mee: shoh
„ bury	မြေမြှုပ်	myay-hmyo*h*k
„ button	အင်္ကျီသီးတပ်	in:jee-*th*ee: tă*h*t
„ buy	ဝယ်	weh
„ call	ခေါ်	hkāw
„ carry	ဆောင်။ ထမ်း	sowng, htă*h*n:
„ — (on head)	ရွက်	yŏŏet
„ catch	ဖမ်းဆီး။ ဖမ်းမိ	hpä*h*n:-zee:, hpă*h*n:-mee
„ change	ပြောင်း။ *intr.* လဲ။ *tr.* လဲလှယ်။	pyowng:, leh, leh-hleh
„ climb	တက်	tet
„ consent	သဘောတူ	thă*h*baw too
„ cook	ချက်	chet
„ cough	ချောင်းဆိုး	chowng: sô*h*:
„ cover	အုပ်။ ဖုံး	o*h*k, hpô*h*n:
„ dance	က	kă*h*
„ decide	ဆုံးဖြတ်	sô*h*n:-hpyă*h*t
„ deny	ငြင်းပယ်	gnyin:-peh
„ depart, go away	ထွက်သွား	htwet-thwā*h*:
„ descend	ဆင်း။ သက်	sin:, thet
„ desire, wish for	လို။ လိုချင်	lo*h*, lo*h*-jin
„ do, make	ပြု။ လုပ်	pyŏŏ, lo*h*k
„ draw, pull	ဆွဲငင်	sweh-gnin
„ dream	အိပ်မက်	ayn-met
„ drink	သောက်	thowk
„ dress	အဝတ်ဝတ်	ă*h*-wŏŏt wŏŏt
„ dwell, live	နေ	nay
„ eat	စား	tsā*h*:
„ endeavour	ကြိုးစား	kyô*h*:-zā*h*:
„ escape	လွတ်	lŏŏt

English	Burmese.	Pronunciation.
To expel	နှင်ထုတ်	hnin-hto*h*k
„ extract	နုတ်	hno*h*k
„ fall	ကျ။ လဲ	kyă*h*, leh
„ feel (by touch)	စမ်း	tsă*h*n:
„ find, feel	တွေ့	twa̤y
„ finish	အစသတ်။ ပြီးစေ	ă*h*-tsă*h* thă*h*t, pyee:-zay
„ follow	လိုက်	lik
„ forbid	မြစ်တား	myit-tā*h*:
„ forget	မေ့လျော့	ma̤y-lyaw̤
„ frighten	ခြောက်လှန့်	chowk-hlă̤*h*n
„ get	ရ။ ရမိ	yă*h*, yă*h*-mĕĕ
„ give	ပေး။ အပ်	pay:, ă*h*t
„ go	သွား	thwā*h*:
„ go in	ဝင်	win
„ go out	ထွက်	htwet
„ govern	အုပ်စိုး	o*h*k-tso*h*:
„ grow	တိုး။ ပွား	tô*h*:, pwā*h*:
„ hang	ဆွဲထား	sweh-htā*h*:
„ hate	မုန်း	mô*h*n:
„ hear	ကြား	kyā*h*:
„ help	မစ	mă*h*-ză*h*
„ hide	ဝှက်ထား	hwet-*h*tā*h*:
„ — (one's-self)	ပုန်းနေ	pô*h*n:-nay
„ hire	ငှါး	hgnā*h*:
„ hold	ကိုင်	king
„ hope for	မျှော်လင့်	hmyāw-li̤ŋ
„ intend	ကြံ	kyă*h*n
„ join, *tr.*	ဆက်	set
„ joke	ကျီစား	kee-zā*h*:

English.	Burmese.	Pronunciation.
To jump	ခုန်။ ခုန်လွှား	hko*h*n, hko*h*n-hlwā*h*:
„ keep	ယူထား	yoo-htā*h*:
„ kill	သတ်	thă*h*t
„ kindle (fire)	မီးညှိ	mee: hnyĕĕ
„ know	သိ	thĕĕ
„ laugh	ရယ်	yeh
„ learn	သင်	thin
„ lend (*or* borrow)	ချေး	chee:
„ let (permit)	အခွင့်ပေး	ă*h*-hkwi̥n pay:
„ let (*or* hire)	ငှါး	hgnā*h*:
„ let go	လွှတ်	hlŏŏt
„ lie down	အိပ်။ တုံးလုံးနေ	ayk, tô*h*n:-lô*h*n: nay
„ lift	ချီ။ မ	chee, mă*h*
„ light	ထွန်း	htoon:
„ listen	နာ	nā*h*
„ live (be alive)	အသက်ရှင်	ă*h*-thet shin
„ lock	သော့ခတ်	thaw̥ hkă*h*t
„ look for	ကြည့်ရှာ	kyee̥-shā*h*
„ loosen	လျှော့	shaw̥
„ lose	အပျောက်ခံ။ ရှုံး	ă*h*-pyowk hkă*h*n, shô*h*n:
„ love	ချစ်	chit
„ mark	မှတ်။ မှတ်ထား	hmă*h*t, hmă*h*t-htā*h*:
„ marry	ထိမ်းမြန်း။ လက်ထပ်	htāyn:-myă*h*n:, let-htă*h*t
„ —(of a woman)	ဆောင်နှင်း။ လက်ထပ်	sowng-hnin:, let-htă*h*t
„ meet	တွေ့ကြုံ	twḁy-kyo*h*n
„ measure	တိုင်းထွာ	ting:-htwā*h*
„ mix	ရောနှော	yaw-hnaw
„ move, *tr.*	ရွှေ့	shwḁy

English.	Burmese.	Pronunciation.
To need, want	လို	loh
„ obey, listen	နားထောင်	nāh: htowng
„ offend	နာစေ။ နှောင့်ရှက်	nāh-zay, hnowṇg-shet
„ open	ဖွင့်	hpwiṇ
„ order, command	အမိန့်ပေး။ မှာထား	ăh-mạyn-pay:, hmāh-htāh:
„ own	ပိုင်	ping
„ — (confess)	ဖြောင့်	hpyowṇg
„ pack up	ထုပ်	htohk
„ pick up	ကောက်	kowk
„ place, put	ထား။ တင်	htāh:, tin
„ — (in)	သွင်း။ ထည့်	thwin:, hteḥ
„ play	ကစား	kăh-zāh:
„ plough	ထွန်	htŏŏn
„ pluck, pick	ဆွတ်	sŏŏt
„ pour out	သွန်း။ လောင်း။ ငှဲ့	thoon:, lowng:, hgneḥ
„ praise	ချီးမွမ်း	chee:-moon:
„ prepare, repair	ပြင်ဆင်	pyin-zin
„ press	နှိပ်။ ဖိ	hnayk, hpĕĕ
„ push	တွန်း။ ထိုး	toon:, htôh:
„ quench	သတ်ဖြေ	thăht-hpyay
„ reach	မှီ	hmee
„ read	ဖတ်	hpăht
„ reap	ရိတ်	yayk
„ receive	လက်ခံ။ ခံယူ	let-hkăhn, hkăhn-yoo
„ reckon, count	ရေတွက်	yay-twet
„ refuse	ငြင်းဆန်	gnyin:-zăhn
„ regret	နှစ်မြော	hnăh-myaw
„ remain	နေ	nay
„ — (behind)	ကျန်ရစ်	kyăhn-yit

English.	Burmese.	Pronunciation.
To remember	မှတ်မိ။ သတိရ	hmă*h*t-mée, thă*h*dēē [yă*h*
,, repay (give [back)	ပြန်ပေး	pyá*h*n-pay:
,, rest	နားနေ။ ရပ်နေ	nā*h*:-nay, yă*h*t-nay
,, retreat [back	ဆုတ်သွား	so*h*k-thwā*h*:
,, return, come	ပြန်လာ	pya*h*n-lā*h*
,, — (go back)	ပြန်သွား	pyă*h*n-thwā*h*:
,, ride	စီး	tsee:
,, rob	လုယူ	lŏŏ-yoo
,, rub	ပွတ်။ တိုက်	pŏŏt, tik
,, run	ပြေး	pyay:
,, save (deliver)	ကယ်ထင်	keh-tin
,, say, tell, speak	ပြော။ ဆို	pyaw, so*h*
,, scatter	ကြဲ။ ဖြန့်	kyeh:, hpyă*h*n̥
,, see	မြင်	myin
,, seek	ရှာ	shā*h*
,, sell	ရောင်း	yowng:
,, serve (as ser- [vant)	အမှုထမ်း	ă*h*-hmŏŏ htă*h*n:
,, sever	ဖြတ်	hpyă*h*t
,, sew, stitch	ချုပ်	cho*h*k
,, shake	လှုပ်	hlo*h*k
,, sharpen	ချွန်	chyŏŏn
,, shave	ဆံရိတ်	să*h*n yayk
,, shine, *intr.*	အရောင်ထွက်	ă*h*-yowng htwet
,, show (point [out)	ပြ။ ပြသ။ ညွှန်ပြ	pyă*h*, pya*h*-thă*h*, [hnyŏŏn-pyă*h*
,, sign (letter, &c.)	လက်မှတ်ထိုး	let-hmă*h*t htô*h*:
,, sit down	ထိုင်	hting
,, slash	ခုတ်	hko*h*k
,, sleep	အိပ်ပျော်	ayk-pyāw

English.	Burmese.	Pronunciation.
To smell, *tr.*	အနံ့ရ။ နမ်း	ă*h*-nă*h*ŋ yă*h*, nă*h*n:
„ —, *intr.*	အနံ့ထွက်	ă*h*-nă*h*ŋ-htwet
„ sneeze	ချေ	chëë
„ sow (seed)	ကြဲ	kyeh
„ spoil, *tr.*	ဖျက်ဆီး	hpyet-see:
„ spread	ခင်းကျင်း	hkin:-kyin:
„ sprinkle	ဖြန်း	hpyă*h*n:
„ squeeze	ညှစ်	hnyit
„ stand	ရပ်	yă*h*t
„ steal	ခိုး။ ခိုးယူ	hkô*h*:, hkô*h*:-yoo
„ surround	ဝန်းရံ	woon:-yă*h*n
„ swallow	မျို	myo*h*
„ swell	ရောင်	yowng
„ swim	ရေကူး	yay koo:
„ take	ယူ	yoo
„ — off	ချွတ်	chŏŏt
„ teach	သင်ချ	thin-chă*h*
„ think	ထင်။ စိတ်ထင်။ မှတ်	htin, tsayt-htin, hmă*h*t
„ throw	ပြစ်	pit
„ — away	စွန့်ပြစ်	tsŏŏŋ-pit
„ touch	ထိ။ တို့	htëë, toh
„ translate	ပြန်ဆို	pyă*h*n zo*h*
„ travel	ခရီးသွား	hkă*h*-yee:-thwā*h*:
„ tread	နင်း	nin:
„ understand	နားလည်	nā*h*: leh
„ unpack	အထုပ်ဖြည်	ă*h*-hto*h*k hpyay
„ use	သုံးဆောင်	thô*h*n:-zowng
„ wail, cry	ငိုကြွေး။ ငို	gno*h*-jway:, gno*h*
„ wash	ဆေး	say:

English.	Burmese.	Pronunciation.
To wash clothes	လျှော်	shāw
„ — the face	မျက်နှာသစ်	myet-hnāh thit
„ weigh, *tr.*	ချိန်	chayn
„ will, be willing	စိတ်ပါ။ သဘောတူ	tsayt-pāh, thăhbaw-too
„ wipe	သုတ်	thohk
„ work	လုပ်	lohk
„ wrap up	ထုပ်ရစ်။ ထုပ်	htohk-yit, htohk
„ write	ရေးသား	yay:-thāh:
„ yield, give way	အားလျှော့	āh: shaw

Auxiliary or Modifying Verbs.

These verbs are chiefly used to modify the mode of the principal verb, and follow between it and the affix of tense.

able, possible, to be	နှိုင် *or* နိုင်	hning *or* ning
accustomed, skilled, to be	တတ်	tăht
at leisure, to be	အား	āh:
attain, to	မှီ	hmee
averse, loth, to be	ပျင်း	pyin:
cause, to	စေ	tsay
come to an end,	ကုန်	kohn
continue [be spent	နေ	nay
cruel, unfeeling, to	ရက်[1]	yet
dare, to [be	ဝံ့	wŏŏn
deserving of, to be	ထိုက်	htik

[1] ရက် yet, with a negative has the force of being '*incapable of*', or '*without the heart*' to do a thing, as မရိုက်ရက်ပူး măh yik-yet-hpoo:, (*I*) *have not the heart to beat* (*him*).

English.	Burmese.	Pronunciation.
desire, to	ချင်။ လို	chin, lo*h*
difficult, to be	ခဲး	hkeh:
direct, to be	တည့်	teḥ
do again, to	ပြန်	pyă*h*n
easy, to be	လွယ်။ သာ	lweh, thā*h*
exceed, to	လွန်း	loon:
happen, to	မိ	mëe
obtain (must)	ရ	yă*h*
practicable, to be	ဖြစ်	hpyit
pretty, to be (very)	လှ	hlá*h*
proper, good, to be	ကောင်း။ သင့်	kowng:, thiņ
revolve (remain)	ရစ်	yit
right, to be (ought)	အပ်	ă*h*'t
shun, to	ဖဲ။ ဘဲ	hpeh, beh
sufficient, to be	လောက်	lowk
suitable, to be	ဖွယ်။ ရာ။ တန်	hpweh, yā*h*, tā*h*n
try, to [to	စမ်း	tsá*h*n:
turn back (repeat),	တုံ့	to*h*ņ

E camples.

Burmese.	Pronunciation.	Principal Verb.	Auxiliary and Affix.	Pronunciation.	Force.
ကုန်	kohn	သေ	ကုန်ပြီ	thay kohn byee	*quite* dead
ကောင်း	kowng:	ပြော	ကောင်းသည်	pyaw-gowng:-*th*ĕĕ	*proper to* say
ချင်	jin	ဝယ်	ချင်သည်	weh jin-*th*ĕĕ	*desire* to buy
စမ်း	tsăhn:	ဖတ်	စမ်းပါ	hpăht tsăhn:-bah	*endeavour* to read
ထတ်	tăht	ဝင်	ထတ်သည်	win dăht-thĕĕ	*accustomed* to enter
ထန်	tăhn	ပြု	ထန်သည်	pyŏŏ dăhn-*th*ĕĕ	*fit* to do
ထိုက်	htăk	သေ	ထိုက်သည်	thay dik-thĕĕ	*worthy* of death
နေ	nay	လုတ်	နေသည်	lohk nay-*th*ĕĕ	*continue* to do
နိုင်	hning	သွား	နိုင်သည်	thwāh: hning-*th*ĕĕ	*able* to go
ပြန်	pyăhn	လာ	ပြန်သည်	lăh byăhn-*th*ĕĕ	*again* comes, return
ရ	yăh	ပြု	ရမည်	pyŏŏ yăh-mĕĕ	*must* (*got* to) do
ရာ	yăh	ခံရ	ရာသည်	hkăhn-yăh yăh-*th*ĕĕ	*should* obtain
လို	loh	ဝယ်	လိုသည်	weh loh *th*ĕĕ	*wish* to buy
လွယ်	lweh	မြင်	လွယ်သည်	myin lweh-*th*ĕĕ	*easy* to see
လောက်	lowk	စား	လောက်သည်	tsăh: lowk-thĕĕ	*sufficient* to eat
လှ	hlăh	များ	လှသည်	myăh: hlăh-*th*ĕĕ	*very* many, to be
ဝံ့	wŏŏn	သွား	ဝံ့သည်	thwāh: wŏŏn-*th*ĕĕ	*dare* to go
သင့်	thin	ယူ	သင့်သည်	yoo *thin-th*ĕĕ	*fit* (ought) to take

Adverbs, Conjunctions, and Prepositions.

English.	Burmese.	Pronunciation.
about (nearly)	ခန့်။ လောက်	hkăhn, lowk
— (concerning)	ဆိုင်၍	sing yŏŏay
above (more than)	ကျော်။ ထက်။ အလွန်	kyāw, det, ăh-lŏŏn
abundantly	ကြွယ်ဝစွာ	kyŏŏeh-wăhzŏŏāh
according to	နှင့်အညီ။ နှင့်အတူ။ အတိုင်	hniṇ ăh-nyee, hniṇ ăh-too, ăh-ting
across	ကန့်လန့်။ ရှောက်	kăhṇ-lăhṇ, showk
afresh	အသစ်	ăh-thit
after	နောက်မှာ	nowk-hmāh
afterwards	နောက်နောင်	nowk-nowng
again	တဖန်	tăh-hpăhn
against (in opposi-	ဆန့်ကျင်ဘက်	săhṇ-jin-bet
ago [tion)	အထက်က	ăh-htet-kăh
all (of)	အားလုံး	āh:-lôhn:
— at once, sud-	ရုပ်ခနဲ	yohkhkăhneh
almost [denly	လု	lŏŏ
alone, solely	ကိုယ်ထီး။ တခုတည်း	koh dee:, tăh-hkŏŏ dee:
aloud	အသံကျယ်လို့	ăh-thăhn kyeh-loḥ
already	အရင်တခါ	ăh-yin tăh-hkāh
also, too	လည်း	lee: [dwin
although	သို့သော်။ သို့ရာတွင်	*thoḥ-thāw*, *thoḥ*-yāh
altogether, quite	အကုန်	ăh-kohn
always	အစဉ်မပြတ်။ အမြဲ	ăh-tsin măh pyăht, ăh-
and (nouns)	နှင့်	hniṇ [myeh
— (verbs)	ရွေ့။ (၍)	yŏŏay
anywhere [about	ဘယ်အရပ်မဆို	beh ăh-yăht măh soh
around, round	ပတ်လည်	paht-leh

English.	Burmese.	Pronunciation.
as	ကဲ့သို့	ge̥h-*th*ŏ*h*
as much, as many	ဤမျှ	ee-hmyă*h*
as soon as, immediately	ချက်ခြင်း	chet-chin:
at	မှာ။ နှိက်။ (၌)	hmā*h*, hnik
at first	အဦးဆုံးမှာ	ă*h*-oo:-zô*h*n:-hmā*h*
at last	နောက်ဆုံးမှာ	nowk-sô*h*n:-hmā*h*
at the most	အများဆုံးမှာ	ă*h*-myā*h*:-zô*h*n:-hmā*h*
at once	တခါတည်း	tă*h*-hkā*h*-dee: (*or* tă*h*-gă*h*-deh:)
at present	ယခုမှာ	yă*h*-hkŏŏ-hmā*h*
because	ကြောင့်။ သော့ကြောင့်	jowng̥g, *th*aw̥ jowng̥g
before (time)	အရင်က	ă*h*-yin-gă*h*
— (place)	အရှေ့မှာ။ ထံ	ă*h*-shay̥-hmā*h*, htă*h*n
behind	နောက်မှာ	nowk-hmā*h*
below, under, beneath	အောက်မှာ	owk-hmā*h*
besides	၎င်ပြင်	lă*h*-gowng:-pyin
better	သာ၍	thā*h*-yŏŏay̥
between	စပ်ကြားမှာ	tsă*h*t-kyā*h*:-hmā*h*
—, among(st)	အတွင်းမှာ	ă*h*-twin:-hmā*h*
beyond	အလွန်မှာ	ă*h*-lŏŏn-hmā*h*
but	သို့ရာတွင်	*th*o̥*h*-yā*h*-dwin
by means of	အားဖြင့်။ ဖြင့်	āh:-hpyin̥, hpyin̥
by the side of	အနားမှာ။ တဖက်မှာ	ă*h*-nā*h*-hmā*h*, tă*h*-bet-hmā*h*
by turns	တလှည့်ကျ	tă*h* hle̥h-jă*h*
certainly	ဧကံအမှန်	aykă*h*n ă*h*-hmă*h*n
close to	ကပ်၍	kă*h*t-yŏŏay̥
consequently	ထိုအကြောင်းကြောင့်	hto*h* ă*h*-kyowng:-jowng̥g
daily	နေ့စဉ်။ နေ့တိုင်း	nḁy-zin, nḁy-ding
doubtless	ဒွိဟမရှိ	dwĕĕ-hă*h* mă*h* shéĕ

English.	Burmese.	Pronunciation.
down (direction)	အောက်သို့	owk-thọ*h*
— (position)	အောက်မှာ	owk-hmā*h*
during	စဉ်တွင်	tsin-dwin
early, betimes	စောစော	tsaw-zaw
either . . . or[1]	လည်းကောင်း—လည်းကောင်း။ ၎င်—၎င်	lă*h*-gowng:—lă*h*-gowng:
elsewhere	အခြားသို့	ăh-chā*h*:-*th*ŏ̤*h*
enough (of)	လောက်အောင်	lowk-owng
even if	ပင်လျှင်	bin-hlyin
everywhere	အရပ်တိုင်း	ă*h*-yă*h*t-ding:
exactly	သေချာစွာ	thay-jā*h*-zŏŏā*h*
exceedingly	သာလွန်စွာ	thā*h*-lŏŏn-zŏŏā*h*
except, *prep.*	ထား၍	htā*h*:-yŏŏ̤ay
far, distant	ဝေးစွာ	way:-zŏŏā*h*
for, *conj.*	အကြောင်းမှာ	ă*h*-kyowng:-hmā*h*
—, *prep.*	အဖို့။ သို့	ă*h*-hpọ*h*, bọ*h*
formerly	အရင်က	ă*h*-yin-gă*h*
forward	ရှေ့သို့	shạy *th*ọ*h*
from	က။ မှ [အစဉ်	gă*h*, hmă*h* [tsin
fully	ထိုက်ရှိုက်။ အကုန်	tik-yik, ă*h*-ko*h*n ă*h*-
hardly	မရှိတရှိ	mă*h*-hmee-dă*h*-hmee
heedlessly, inad- [vertently	အမှတ်တမဲ့	ă*h*-hmă*h*t tă*h*-mẹh
here	သည်မှာ	dee-hmā*h*
herewith	သည်နှင့်တကွ	*th*ee-hniṇ tă*h*-gwă*h*
hitherto	ယခုတိုင်အောင်	yă*h*-hkŏŏ tiṇg-owng
how, like	သည်ကဲ့သို့	*th*ee gẹh-*th*ŏ̤*h*

[1] NOTE.—လည်းကောင်း — လည်းကောင်း commonly written ၎င် — ၎င် is used for '*either — or*' and '*both — and*'. ၎င်း by itself is used for '*the aforesaid*' or '*ditto*'. နှိုက် hnik is usually written ၌ and ရွေ့ yöögy ၍.

English.	Burmese.	Pronunciation.
how much ?	ဘယ်လောက်	beh-lowk
however	သို့သော်လည်း	*thŏh-th*āw-lee:
if	လျှင်	hlyin
in	တွင်။ ၌	dwin, hnik
in front, before	အရှေ့က	ă*h*-shay-gă*h*
in future	နောင်ကာလ	nowng-kā*h*lā*h*
in order to	ငှါ။ ရအောင်	*h*gnā*h*, yā*h*-owng
in the midst of	အလယ်၌	ă*h*-leh-hnik
indeed	အကယ်၍	ă*h*-keh-yŏŏay
inside	အတွင်းတွင်။ ထဲမှာ	ă*h*-twin:-dwin, deh-hmā*h*
instead of	အစား	ă*h*-tsā*h*:
into	ထဲသို့	deh-*th*o*h*
just as	သကဲ့သို့	thă*h*-geh-*th*o*h*
just now	ယခင်	yă*h*-hkin
lately	တနေ့က	tă*h*-nay-gă*h*
less	သာ၍ငယ်	thā*h*-yŏŏay gneh
likewise	ထိုနည်းတူ	hto*h*-nee:-doo
little by little	စိုးစဉ်း	zô*h*:-zin:
long ago	လွန်လေပြီးသောအခါ	lŏŏn-lay-byee:-*th*aw ă*h*-hkā*h*
merely	သက်သက်	thet-thet
more	သာ၍	thā*h*-yŏŏay
moreover	၎င်ပြင်	lĕe:-gowng:-pyin
much	များစွာ	myā*h*:-zŏŏā*h*
mutually	အချင်းချင်း	ă*h*-chin:-jīn:
near	အနီးသို့	ă*h*-nee:-*th*o*h*
never	တခါမျှမ	tă*h*-hkā*h*-hmyă*h*-mă*h*
nevertheless, notwithstanding	မဟုတ်သော်လည်း	mă*h*-ho*h*k thāw-lee:
next to	အနီးဆုံး	ă*h*-nee-zô*h*n:

English.	Burmese.	Pronunciation.
not	မ	mă*h*
not at all	အလျှင်းမဟုတ်	ă*h*-hlyin: mă*h*-ho*h*k
not yet	မဟုတ်သေး	mă*h* ho*h*k thay:
now	ယခု	yă*h*-hkŏŏ
nowadays	ယခုအခါ	yă*h*-hkŏŏ ă*h*-hkā*h*
nowhere	ဘယ်မှာမဟုတ်	beh-hmā*h* mă*h*-ho*h*k
of	၏	ëë (abbreviated form of ဧည် which is never [used)
off	အပေါ်က	ă*h*-pāw-gă*h*
often	အကြိမ်ကြိမ်	á*h*-kyayn:-jayn:
on, upon	အပေါ်မှာ	ă*h*-pāw-hmā*h*
on account of	ကြောင့်	jyowng
on the left	လက်ဝဲဖက်	let-weh-bet
on the right	လက်ယာဖက်	let-yā*h*-bet
once	တခါတည်း။ တလီ	tă*h*-gă*h*-de*h*:, tă*h*-lee
only	သာ	*th*ā*h*
opposite	မျက်နှာချင်းဆိုင်	myet-hnā*h*-chin:-zing
or, otherwise	သို့မဟုတ်	*th*o*h*-mă*h*-ho*h*k
outside, out of	အပြင်မှာ	ă*h*-pyin-hmā*h*
over (above)	အထက်မှာ	ă*h*-htet-hmā*h*
possibly	ဖြစ်ကောင်းဖြစ်မည်	hpyit-kowng: hpyit [meë
presently	ယခုပင်	yă*h*-hkŏŏ-bin
probably	ဟုတ်ကောင်းဟုတ် [မည်	ho*h*k-kowng: ho*h*k- [meé
purposely	ထမင်	htă*h*-min
quickly	အလျင်။ မြန်မြန်	ă*h*-lyin, myă*h*n-myá*h*n
rather, preferably	သာ၍အလိုရှိသည်နှင့်	thā*h*-yŏŏay ă*h*-lo*h* shëë-*th*ëë-hning
—, somewhat	ခတ်။ တော်တော်	hkă*h*t, tāw-dāw
repeatedly	အဖန်တလဲလဲ	á*h*-hpá*h*n-tá*h*-leh-leh

English.	Burmese.	Pronunciation.
save, excepting	ထား၍	htāh:-yŏŏg̥ay
since, *prep.*	နောက်	nowk
—, *conj.*	သို့ဖြစ်၍	*th*o̥h-hpyit-yŏŏg̥ay
so, thus	ထိုသို့	hto*h*-*th*o̥*h*
so much	ဤမျှ။ ထိုမျှ	ee-hmyă*h*, hto*h*-hmyă*h*
some	တစုံတခုသော	tă*h*-zo*h*n tă*h*-hkŏŏ-thaw
somehow	တစုံတခုသောနည်းအားဖြင့်	tă*h*-zo*h*n-tă*h* hkŏŏ-*th*aw nee:-āh:-hpyin̥
sometimes	တခါတလေ	tă*h*-hkā*h* tă*h*-lay
soon	များမကြာ	myā*h*: mă*h*-kyā*h*
straightway	ချက်ချင်း။ အခြားမဲ့	chet-chin:, ă*h*-chā*h*: meh̥
suddenly	ရုတ်ခနဲ	yo*h*k-hkă*h*-neh
sufficiently	လောက်အောင်	lowk-owng
that, *conj.*	အောင်	owng
then	ထိုအခါ၌	hto*h* ă*h*-hkā*h*-hnik
thence	ထိုက	ho*h*-gă*h*
thenceforth	ထိုမှစ၍	hto*h*-hmă*h* tsă*h*-yŏŏg̥ay
there	ထိုမှာ	ho:-hmā*h*
therefore	ထိုကြောင့်	hto*h*-jowng̥
throughout	တရှောက်လုံး	tă*h*-showk-lô*h*n:
— (by means of)	အားဖြင့်	ă*h*:-hpyin̥
till, until	တိုင်အောင်	ting-owng
to	သို့။ ကို။ အား	tho̥*h*, ko*h*, ā*h*:
together with	နှင့်အတူ	hnin̥-ă*h*-too
too, also	လည်း	lee:
too much	လွန်း	loon:
towards	သို့။ ဆီသို့	tho̥*h*, see-*th*o̥*h*
under	အောက်မှာ	owk-hmā*h*
unexpectedly	အမှတ်မထင်	ă*h*-hmă*h*t mă*h*-htin

English.	Burmese.	Pronunciation.
unless	မ — လျှင်	măh (*verb*) hlyin
up, upwards	အပေါ်သို့။ အထက်သို့	ăh-pāw-*th*ọ*h*, ăh-htet-thọ*h*
— (of river)	ညာသို့	nyā*h*-*th*ọ*h*
weekly	ခုနှစ်ရက်တကြိမ်	hkŏŏ-hnă*h*-yet tă*h*-jayn:
well	ကောင်းကောင်း	kowng:-gowng:
when ?	ဘယ်သောအခါလဲ	beh-*th*aw-ă*h* - hkă*h* leh (*or* beh-do*h*-gā*h* leh)
whence ?	ဘယ်ကလဲ။ ဘယ်ဆီကလဲ	beh-gă*h* leh, beh-zee-gă*h* leh
where ?	ဘယ်မှာလဲ။ ဘယ်ဆီမှာလဲ	beh-hmā*h* leh, beh-zee-hmā*h* leh
wherever (*pre-ceded by a verb*)[1]	လေရာရာ	lay-yā*h*-yā*h*
whereupon	ထိုသို့ဖြစ်၍	htọ*h*-*th*ọ*h*-hpyit-yŏŏay
whether, if	ဖြစ်စေ	hpyit-tsay
while, whilst	တုံးခါ။ ရှိစဉ်ကာလ	dô*h*n:-gā*h*, shēē-zin-kā*h*lă*h*
why ?	ဘယ့်နှယ်ကြောင့်လဲ။ ဘာပြုလို့လဲ	beh-hneh-jowṇg leh, bā*h*-pyŏŏ-lọ*h* leh
willingly	သဘောတူစွာ	thă*h*baw-too-zŏŏā*h*
wisely	လိမ္မာစွာ	laymmā*h*-zŏŏā*h*
with	နှင့်။ နှင့်တကွ	hniṇ, hniṇ-tă*h*-gwă*h*
— (by means of)	နှင့်။ ဖြင့်	hniṇ, hpyiṇ
without (absent)	မရှိဘဲ။ မပါဘဲ	mă*h*-shēē-beh, mă*h*-pā*h*-beh (*any other verb can be substituted for* shēē *or* pā*h*)
— (outside)	ပြင်မှာ။ ပမှာ	pyin-hmā*h*, pă*h*-hmā*h*
yearly	နှစ်စဉ်	hnit-tsin
yet (*conj.*)	သို့သော်လည်း	*th*ọ*h*-*th*āw-lee:
—, *adv.*)	သေး	*thay:* (*follows the verb*)

[1] A-, သွားလေရာရာ thwā*h*:-lay-yā*h*-yā*h*, *wherever (he) goes.*

OUTLINES OF BURMESE GRAMMAR.

THE NOUN.

Gender.

All nouns in Burmese are without gender unless they have the affix denoting male or female attached.

The feminine affix is always မ măh.

The masculine affix varies.

ခွေး hkway, *dog*; ခွေးမ hkway:măh, *dog* (female); ခွေးထီး hkway:dee:, *dog* (male).

ကြက် kyet, *fowl*; ကြက်မ kyetmăh, *hen*; ကြက်ဖ kyet hpăh, *cock.*

For human beings there are a few differences; thus,

လူ loo, *man*; ယောကျ်ား yowkyāh:, *a man* (as distinguished from woman); မိန္မ mayn:măh, *woman.*

In some cases it is only necessary to designate the female; as,

ကျွန် kyŏŏn, *a slave*; ကျွန်မ kyŏŏn-măh, *a female slave* or *servant.*

ရွာသား yŏŏăh-thāh:, *a villager* (male).

ရွာသူ yŏŏăh-thoo, *a villager* (female).

မင်း min:, *a governor*; မင်းကတော် Min:kăhdāw, *a governor's lady.*

Classification of Nouns.

Nouns may be divided into three classes: 1. Simple, 2. Abstract, 3. Compound.

1. The simple noun is a monosyllable denoting some object.

2. The abstract or verbal noun is formed from a verb-root by prefixing the syllable ăh; thus,

V. လုပ် lohk, *to do, make.* N. အလုပ် ăh-lohk, *work.*

V. ရာ yāh, *to be suitable.* N. အရာ ăh-yāh, *what is suitable, a thing, place.*

Note.—It is commonly stated that there are other formations, such as ခြင်း chin:, ချက် chet, ဖွယ် hpweh, but as a matter of fact it is not so, for these affixes are themselves merely abstract nouns which have dropped the ah in composition; thus, ပြုခြင်း pyŏŏ-jin: is ပြု pyŏŏ (*to do*) + ăh-chin: (*action*) which has been derived from the verb kyiṉ, *to do.* It may be said that there is no verb kyin: (*to do*), but the rules of the language allow of a verb hkyin (or chin) (*to be done*), though it is now obsolete.

3. The compound noun is formed by uniting verbs and nouns in various ways; thus,

ရွာ yŏŏāh, *a village* + သား thāhs, *son* = villager.

လမ်း lăhn:, *a road* + ပြ pyăh, *to show* = guide.

နေ nay, *to dwell* + အိမ် ayn, *a house* = a dwelling-house.

ထိုင် hting, *to sit* + အရာ (ăh)-yāh, *place* = a seat.

မြင်း myins, *horse* + စီး tsee, *to ride* + သူ thoo, *person* + ရဲ yeh, *bold* = a horse-soldier.

To the above classes must be added a class containing nouns adapted and taken from other languages.

Number.

The plural of nouns is formed, when necessary, by adding များ myā*h*: (*to be many*), or တို့ dọ*h* (a short form of တိုး to*h*:, *to increase*), or the two combined. တို့ dọ*h* is generally connected with animate beings. Thus,

အိမ် ayn, *a house*; အိမ်များ ayn-myā*h*:, *houses.*

လူ loo, *a man*; လူများ loo-myā*h*: or လူတို့ loo-dọ*h*, *men.*

An indefinite plural is also formed by reduplication of the noun; thus,

အမျိုး ă*h*-myô*h*:, *a kind*; အမျိုးမျိုး ă*h*-myô*h*:-myô*h*:, *various kinds.*

အရပ် ă*h*-yă*h*t, *a place*; အရပ်ရပ် ă*h*-yă*h*t-yă*h*t, *various places.*

Case.

The sign of the nominative case is သည် *th*ĕĕ and follows the noun but is often dispensed with.

ခွေးသည် hkway:*th*ĕé, *a dog* or *the dog.*

All other cases are denoted by affixes of case, which are sometimes called 'postpositions'. They are,

Objective ကို go*h*.

Genitive ၏ ĕĕ, *of* (generally omitted).

Dative အား ā*h*:, *to*; ငှါ hngā*h*, *for*; သို့ thọ*h*, *to*; ကို go*h*, *to.*

Ablative က gă*h*, မှ hmă*h*, *from*; နှင့် hniṇ, *together with.*

Instrumentative နှင့် hniṇ, *with*; ဖြင့် hpyiṇ, *by means of*; ကြောင့် kyowṇg, *on account of, because of.*

Locative တွင် twin, *in*; နိုက် hnik, *at*; မှာ hmā*h*, *at, as regards*; ဝယ် weh, *at.*

NOTE.—နိုက် hnik is usually written ၌.

Besides the above simple affixes of case, there are a number of auxiliary words used between the noun and the affix in order to denote more clearly relationship or position.

Being verbal nouns, their real form would have the verbal အ ăh prefixed, but in composition this is omitted.

အိမ် ပေါ် မှာ ayn-bāw-hmāh, house (of) upper part-at = *upon the house.*

အိမ်ပြင်မှ ayn-byin-hmăh, house-outside-from = *from outside the house.*

A list of these is given at p. 97.

The sign ၏ ēē has been given as the genitive but it is usually dispensed with, the first of two nouns being (except when in apposition) in the genitive case and always pronounced with an abrupt tone, which is sometimes denoted by the sharp or abrupt accent ့, which kills even the heavy accent း; thus,

မင်း၏ဘဏ္ဍာ min:-ēē-hbăhndāh (king-of-property) becomes min̥:-hpăhdāh, *the king's property.*

THE PRONOUN.

There are five primitive personal pronouns.

Sing.	ငါ gnāh, *I.*	*Plur.*	ငါတို့ gnāh-doh or တို့ doh, *we.*
	သင် thin, *thou.*		သင်တို့ thin-doh, *ye.*
	မင်း min:, *thou.*		မင်းတို့ min:-doh, *ye.*
	နင် nin, *thou.*		နင်တို့ nin-doh, *ye.*
	သူ thoo, *he, she.*		သူတို့ thoo-doh, *they.*

It is rude to use ငါ gnāh and နင် nin, so, for the sake of politeness, a number of other forms are in general use.

For *I* the usual form is ကျွန်ုပ် kyŏŏn-ohk, *humble servant.*

Sometimes it is အကျွန်ုပ် ă*h*-kyŏŏn-o*h*k, and for a woman ကျွန်မ kyŏŏn-mă*h*, shortened to ကျမ kyă*h*-mă*h*.

ကျွန်တော် kyŏŏn-däw, *your royal slave*, and ကျွန်တော်မျိုး kyŏŏn-dāw-myô*h*:, *your race of royal slaves*, is used by persons petitioning a person in authority.

For *thou* or *you* the common form is မောင်မင်း mowng-min:.

Speaking to some one older than one's-self one would use ခင်ဗြား hkin-byā*h*:, *Mr.*, *Sir.*

To a priest or some one in authority ကိုယ်တော် kô*h*-dāw.

The third person သူ thoo (literally *person*) is always used for male or female but, if necessary, သူမ thoo-mă*h* may be used for *she*.

Terms of politeness in general use are given at p. 127.

The Relative Pronoun.

There is no relative pronoun like *Who*, but the position is expressed by a participial form of the verb; thus, စာသင် သော သူ tsā*h*-thin-*th*aw thoo, writing-teaching-person = *the person who teaches*, or လမ်းရှောက်သွားသော သူ lă*h*n:-showk-thwā*h*:-*th*aw-thoo, road-pass along-going-person, *the man who is going along the road.*

In this last example the participial သော thaw (or sometimes သည့် thẹe) is used with two verbs: others might be added.

The Reflexive Pronoun.

ကိုယ်တိုင် kô*h*-ding, or ကိုယ် kô*h*, *self*; thus,

ငါကိုယ်တိုင် gnā*h*-kô*h*-ding, or rather ကျွန်ုပ်ကိုယ်တိုင် kyŏŏn-o*h*k-kô*h*-ding, *I myself.*

မိမိ mĕĕmĕĕ, *one's-self, himself, herself*; thus,

မိမိခွေး mĕĕmĕĕ hkway:, *one's own dog.*

The Interrogative Pronoun.

ဘယ် (or အဘယ်) beh (ă*h*-beh) or beh.

ဘယ်သူ beh-*th*oo, *Who?*

ဘာ bā*h* (contr. for ဘယ်ဟာ beh-hā*h*), *What?*

ဘယ်သင်း beh-*th*in:, *Which?*

ဘယ်လောက် beh-lowk, *How much?*

ဘယ်နှစ် beh-hnit, *How many?*[1]

The Negative.

'No one' is expressed by using the Int. pronoun with မျှ hmyă*h*, *even*, and မ mă*h*, *not*; thus,

ဘယ်သူမျှမရှိ beh *th*oo hmyă*h* mă*h* shĕĕ, Who even not is = *There is no one.*

ကျွန်ုပ်ဘာမျှမလုပ်ဖူး kyŏŏno*h*k bā*h* hmyă*h* mă*h* lo*h*k hpoo: I what even not do = *I am doing nothing.*

The affix ဖူး hpoo: is a strong one often used with မ mă*h*.

The Demonstrative Pronoun.

ဤ ee သည် *th*ee	*this.*	ထို hto*h* ဟို ho*h* ယင်း yin:	*that.*

သည် and ထို are colloquial, and always precede the noun; as,

သည် ကြောင် *th*ee kyowng, *this cat.*

ထိုဝက် hto*h* wet, *that pig.*

[1] ဘယ်နှစ် beh-hnit (final t scarcely pronounced) can never stand alone but is always preceded by the subject of inquiry and followed by the proper numeral affix (pp. 79–81); thus, မြင်းဘယ်နှစ်ကောင်ရှိသလဲ myin: beh-hnit kowng shĕĕ-thă*h*-leh, horses how many animals are there? = *How many horses are there?*

The Compound Relative.

မည်သူမဆို mee-*th*oo-mă*h*-soh, what-person-not-say, *whosoever.*

မည်သည့်အရာမဆို mee-thëë-ă*h*yā*h*-mă*h*-so*h*, what-thing-not-say, *whatsoever.*

မည် is an old form of ဘယ်.

THE ADJECTIVE.

There are a few imported adjectives which have been taken from the Pali and which do not follow the general rule, but the real adjective is the verb-root which may be used before or after the noun ; thus,

ကောင်းသောလူ kowng:-*th*aw-loo လူကောင်း loo-gowng:	*a good man.*

Adjectives imported from other languages and a few anomalous Burmese forms are always placed before the noun, without the conjunctive particle သော *th*aw ; thus,

မဟာ မင်း ကြီး mă*h*hā*h* min: jee:, *a governor of a province.*

မဟာ mă*h*hā*h* is a Pali word meaning *great,* မင်း min: is a person in authority, and ကြီး kyee:, the Burmese *to be great,* used as an adjective.

The Comparison of Adjectives.

The comparative is made by the use of the verb သာ thā*h*, *to surpass* or *exceed,* coupled to the descriptive word by the conjunction ရွေ yŏŏay (always written ၍) ; thus,

သာ၍ကြီးသောအိမ် thā*h*-yŏŏay kyee:-*th*aw ayn, *a surpassing large house, a larger house.*

The Superlative degree is formed by prefixing အ ă*h*, to the verb and adding ဆုံး sô*h*n:, *to be extreme*; thus,

နွားအငယ်ဆုံး nwā*h*:-ă*h*-gneh-zô*h*n:, *the smallest ox.*

The Numeral Adjective.

Cardinals. A list of these is given on p. 78, and here it will be sufficient to show how they are used. They run from one to ten and are perfectly regular. The word for ten, however, is used as a demonstrative affix.

The Burmese cannot say as we do 'one ox', but are obliged to use a descriptive affix (see pp. 79–81) after the number; thus, instead of saying 'one ox', they must say 'ox one animal', and so on till they come to ten, when the affix for animal (or whatever it may be) is dropped and the affix for ten takes its place; after that the affix of kind is used again till the next ten is reached, and so on to one hundred, when a new numeral affix denoting 'hundred' comes in; thus,

ယောက် yowk, being the affix for *man*; we have

လူတယောက် loo tă*h* yowk, man-one-man.

လူငါးယောက် loo gnā*h*: yowk, man-five-men.

လူတဆယ် loo tă*h* seh, man-one-ten.

လူတဆယ်နှင့်တယောက် loo tă*h* seh hniṉ tă*h* yowk, man-one-ten-with-one-man, eleven-men.

And so on till twenty, when it is

လူနှစ်ဆယ် loo hni(t) seh, man-two-ten.

လူနှစ်ဆယ်နှင့်တယောက် loo hni(t) seh hniṉ tă*h* yowk, men-two-tens-and-one-man, *twenty-one men.*

The နှင့် hniṉ (and, with) is often dropped.

Ordinals. Up to ten the Pali ordinals are in general use, but after that one must have recourse to the verb မြှောက် myowk, *to raise*; thus,

တဆယ့်သုံးမြှောက်သောလှေ tă*h* seh thô*hn*ះ myowk thaw hlay, *the 13th boat.*

THE VERB.

The verb is a monosyllable without any particular form and never changes. It may be transitive or intransitive.

Transitives are often formed from intransitives by aspirating the initial consonant; as, ပျက် pyet, *to be destroyed*; ဖျက် hpyet, *to destroy.*

Verb-roots may be strung together so as to form a complete idea; as, ထောင်းထုပုတ်ခတ်သည် htowngះ-htŏŏ-po*h*k-hkă*h*t-thĕĕ, *to give a good beating.* All the verbs signify a different way of hitting.

Sometimes a noun and a verb are compounded to form one idea; thus, *to be glad* is expressed by ဝမ်း woonះ, *the belly* + မြှောက် myowk, *to be raised.*

The Plural.

There are two affixes, ကြ kyă*h* and ကုန် ko*h*n, to express the plural number, but they are not often used; thus,

သူတို့သွားကြသည် thoodŏ*h* thwā*h*ះ-jyă*h*-*th*ëė, *they (are) going.*

Voice, Moods, and Tenses.

Voice, moods, and tenses have to be expressed by affixes (which were once verbs) and auxiliary verbs.

Voice.

The passive voice is formed by the verb ခံ hkă*h*n, *to bear* or *suffer*, with the principal verb in a noun form; thus,

ရိုက် yik, *to beat.*

အရိုက် ခံသည် ă*h*-yik hkă*h*n *th*ěě, a beating to bear, i. e. *to be beaten.*

Moods.

The verb-root by itself may be Infinitive or Imperative.

All other moods, except the Indicative, are shown by auxiliary verbs signifying power, permission, &c.

The *Indicative* Mood is denoted by affixes of time.

Present T.	သည် *th*ěě.	Future	အံ့မည် ă*h*n měě.
	၏ ěě.		လတ္တံ့ (or လတ်အံ့) lă*h*t ă*h*n.
Past	ပြီ pyee.	Pluperfect	ခဲ့ပြီ geḥ-byee.
Future	မည် měě.		ဘူးပြီ hboo:-byee.
	အံ့ ă*h*ṇ.	Past Perf.	နှင့်ပြီ hniṇ-byee.

Though the simple root can be used *Imperatively*, there is a large number of modifying affixes: ချေ chay, လော့ law̥, and တော့ taw̥, simply imply command.

နှင့် hniṇ, and လင့် liṇ, used after မ mă*h*, *not,* are prohibitive.

ပါ pā*h* is entreating and always used in polite language, either by itself or with other affixes.

စေ tsay is causative or precative as သွားစေ thwā*h*:-zay *let him go.* စို့ tso*ḥ*, used only for 1st pers. plur., as သွားကြစို့ thwā*h*: jyă*h*-zo̥, *let us go.*

ခဲ့ hkeḥ is generally used with the verb လာ lā*h*, *to come,* and implies motion towards one's-self.

လိုက် lik (to follow) is harsh and implies motion from.

ဦး ô*h*ng: is an affix that signifies return or recurrence; as, ပေးပါဦး pay: bā*h* ô*h*n:, *please give (it me) again.*

သွားဦးတော့ thwā*h*: ô*h*n: daw̥, *go and return,* used for 'good-bye'.

INTERROGATIVE.

The Burmese do not alter the tone of the voice when asking a question, but use certain affixes, at the end of the sentence, with a tone of assertion.

လော law, and နည်း nee:, are those used formally in writing, but colloquially လား lā*h*:, and လဲ leh, are used ; လား lā*h*: is used for all ordinary questions ; as,

သင်ပြုမည်လား *th*in pyŏŏ mĕĕ lā*h*:, thou do will ? = *will you do it ?*

But if the sentence begins with the interrogative pronoun ဘယ် beh, *who*, or any of its compounds, then လဲ leh *must* be used ; as,

ဘယ်မှာရှိသလဲ beh hmā*h* shĕĕ *th*ă*h* leh, *where is (it)* ?

တုံး dô*h*n: is also used colloquially in place of လဲ leh.

THE USE OF THE NEGATIVE.

The only word for *not* is မ mă*h*, and it immediately precedes the principal verb ; thus,

ကျွန်ုပ်မသွားချင်ဘူး kyŏŏno*h*k mă*h* thwā*h*: jin boo:, I not go wish, *I do not wish to go.*

The boo: at the end is a strong assertive affix generally used with *not*, and if the sense of *never* is required စ tsă*h* must be placed before it :—

ငါမသွားစဖူး gnā*h* mă*h* thwā*h*: ză*h* hpoo:, *I never went.* To make it still stronger we may double the ဖူး and say မသွားစဖူးဘူး mă*h* thwā*h*: ză*h* hpoo: boo:

Before is expressed by placing မှီ hmee, and ခင် hkin, *after* the verb ; thus,

မရောက်မှီ mă*h* yowk hmee, *before (he) arrived*

မပြောခင် mă*h* pyaw gin, *before (he) spoke.*

Without is expressed by placing ဘဲ beh after the verb; thus,
မပြုဘဲ mă*h* pyŏŏ beh, *without doing* (*it*).

Yes and *No*. There is no direct negative like the English *No*, but the verb ဟုတ် ho*h*k, *to be true*, is used; thus,

ဟုတ်သည် ho*h*k *th*ĕĕ, or ဟုတ်ကဲ့ ho*h*k-keh̥, *it is true, yes.*

မဟုတ်ဖူး mă*h* ho*h*k hpoo:, *it is not true, no.*

ပြုအပ်သည်မဟုတ် pyŏŏ a*h*t *th*ĕĕ mă*h* ho*h*k, do proper to not true, *it is not proper to do.*

ORATIO OBLIQUA.

This is shown by the verb ဟူ hoo, *to say*, followed by the verbal conjunction ၍ yŏ̥ay and a verb expressive of saying or thinking. Generally the speaker is designated first followed by the ablative postposition က kă*h*; thus,

သူကမကောင်းဘူးဟူ၍ဆိုသည် thoo gă*h* — mă*h* kawng: boo: — hoo yŏ̥ay so*h* *th*ĕĕ, him from — not good — saying says, i. e. *he says* (*or said*) *it is not good.*

Sometimes instead of ဟူ၍ the short form of the verb ဟူ hoo is used without ၍, as

သူကမလာနိုင်ဟုမှတ်သည် thoo gă*h* mă*h* lā*h* hning hŏŏ — hmat thĕĕ, him from—not come able—say thinks, *he thinks* (*that*) *he cannot come.*

In conversation လို့ lo̥*h* is used instead of ဟု hŏŏ, and sometimes the sentence is still further shortened by the use of တည့် deh̥; thus,

သူလာမည်တည့် thoo lā*h* mëë — deh̥, *he will come he says.*

This တည့် deh̥ is simply a short form for သည် *th*ĕĕ, the assertive affix of the omitted verb ဆို so*h*, *to say*, or ပြော pyaw, *to speak.*

THE SUBSTANTIVE VERB.

There are two substantive verbs,—

ဖြစ် hpyit, *to be, to exist.*

ရှိ shĕĕ, *to be*, which is used in the sense of 'have', the postpositions 'to' or 'at' being expressed or understood, as, သူ့ရှိသည် thoo-shĕĕ-*th*ĕĕ = သူ့မှာရှိသည် thoo-hmā*h* shĕĕ-*th*ĕĕ, *to him there is*, or *he has.*

Thus,

လူတယောက်ရှိသည် loo ta*h*-yowk shĕĕ-*th*ĕĕ, man one(there) is.

သူ့မှာရှိသည် thoo-hmā*h* shĕĕ-*th*ĕĕ, to him is, or, he has.

သင်လူမိုက်ဖြစ်သည် *th*in loo-mik hpyit-thĕĕ, you a fool are.

THE HONORIFIC FORM.

The honorific form is used for very high personages and consists of တော် tāw, the honorific affix, and မူ moo, *to do*; thus,

မင်းကြီးရောက်တော်မူပြီ min:-jee: yowk tāw moo byee, *the governor has arrived.*

In this case မူ moo is considered the principal verb, and to make the negative, မ mă*h* must precede it and the final affix be left out; thus,

ရောက်တော်မမူ yowk tāw mă*h* moo, (*the governor*) *does not arrive*, or *has not arrived.*

CONTINUATIVE AFFIXES.

These take the place of the participle and join clause to clause in a sentence.

၍ yŏŏay and လျက် lyet are what we call present.

လျှင် hlyin and သော် *th*āw are what we call past.

ပြေလျက်သွားသည် pyay lyet thwā*h*: *thēē*, *running* (*he*) *goes.*

ကျားကိုက်၍ရသော်၊ စားကြမည် kyā*h*: kik-yŏŏay yă*h*-thāw-tsā*h*:-jyă*h*-mēē, tiger biting having-got (we) shall eat, i.e. (*we*) *shall eat* (*what we*) *got from the tiger's killing.*

တတ်ကြပြီးလျှင်၊ ပြန်ကြသည် tă*h*t-kyă*h* byee:-hlyin၊ pyă*h*n-jyă*h*-*th*ĕé, skilled (pl.) having-finished (they) returned, i.e. *having completed their education they returned* (*home*).

EUPHONIC AFFIXES.

These are used after verbal roots in conjunction with affixes of mood, tense, and number, but they can be dispensed with, and it is impossible to lay down rules as to their use. The commonest are လေ lay, ချေ chyay, လတ် lă*h*t, ခဲ့ khẹh.

Examples.

လေ lay is one of the most common. It is almost always used in the future compounded with the future affixes အံ့ ă*h*ṇ and မည် mēē, and takes the form of လိမ့်မည် layṃmēē (လေ အံ့ မည်). It is frequently used with the past tense; သွားပြီ thwā*h*: byce, (*he*) *has gone*, is correct, but သွားလေပြီ thwā*h*: lay byee is better.

ပါ pā*h*, the polite affix, is in constant use: it is correct to say သွားတော့ thwā*h*: daw, *go*; but သွားပါတော့ thwā*h*: bā*h* daw is better. ချေ chay is sometimes used with future အံ့ ă*h*ṇ and becomes ချိမ့် chaym, as သူနှင့်အတူသွားချေသော်၊ပျောက်ရချိမ့်မည် thoo hniṇ ă*h*-too thwā*h*: jay *th*āw pyowk yă*h* jayṇ mēē, *If he goes with* (*h'm*) *he must be lost*: both *jay* and *jayṇ* have no meaning and may be omitted, they merely round off the sentence. So, in သူပါကိုပုတ်လိုက်ချေသည် thŏŏ pā*h*-go*h* po*h*k lik chay *thĕĕ*, *(he) smote his cheek*, both လိုက် lik and ချေ chay have really no effect.

လိုက် lik (lit. *follow*) is not always euphonic but conveys a certain amount of meaning and is used with transitive verbs.

လတ် lă*h*t is common and mostly used with သော် thāw; as သွားလတ်သော် thwā*h*: lă*h*t thāw, *having gone*. It gives the idea of 'happened'. Sometimes with fut. အံ့ ă*h*n; as, လတ္တံ့ lă*h*ttă*h*n; သွား လတ္တံ့ *will go (probably)*.

CLOSING AFFIXES.

These are used occasionally at the end of a sentence to give it stronger force. The principal are,—

တည်း dee: = subst. verb ရှိသည် shĕĕ-*thĕĕ*, *to be, is*. Not used colloquially.

စွ tsŏŏă*h* *or* zŏŏă*h* intensifying.

နော် nāw, soliciting acquiescence, as သွားတော့မည်နော် thwā*h*: daw mĕĕ nāw, *I will go, shall I?*

ပေါ့ paw, implies 'of course' in answer to a question. သွားမည်လား thwā*h*: mĕĕ lā*h*, *Are you going?* သွားမည်ပေါ့ thwā*h*: mĕĕ paw, *I shall go, of course.*

THE VERB USED AS A NOUN.

The verb may be used either in its radical form or with its affixes of mood and tense as a noun, and in such cases is governed by postpositions; as,

ပြေးသည်ကိုမြင်လျှင် pyay-*thĕĕ*-go*h* myin-hlyin, runs-to-see-if, *having seen the running*.

ထွက်ပြီးမှ htwet pyee:-hma*h*, come-out-finish from, i.e. *after (he) had come out.*

THE ADVERB.

The adverb proper ends in စွာ zŏŏāh, but there are six different kinds of adverbs. Those in common use are given on pp. 100–106.

MODEL OF VERB.

Infinitive လုပ်သည် lohk-thĕĕ, *to make.*

Indic. Pres. ငါလုပ်သည် gnāh lohk-thĕĕ, *I make,* or,
ငါလုပ်နေသည် gnāh lohk nay-*thĕĕ*, *I am making.*

Past ငါလုပ်ခဲ့သည် gnāh lohk-hkeh-*thĕĕ*, *I made.*

Pres. Perf. ငါလုပ်ပြီ gnāh lohk pyee, *I have made.*

Past Perf. ငါလုပ်ဖူးပြီ gnāh lohk-hpoos-byee, *I had made.*

Future ငါလုပ်မည် gnāh lohk-mëë, *I will make.*

Fut. Perf. ငါလုပ်ပြီးလိမ့်မည် gnāh lohk-pyees-laym-mĕĕ, *I shall have made.*

Potent. Pres. ငါလုပ်နိုင်သည် gnāh lohk hning-*thĕĕ*, *I can make.*

Potent. Perf. ငါလုပ်နိုင်ပြီ gnāh lohk hning-byee, *I could have made.*

Potent. Past Perf. ငါလုပ်ကောင်းပြီ gnāh lohk kowngs-byee, *I might have made.*

Imperative လုပ်တော့ lohk-taw, *make.*
လုပ်စေ lohk-tsay, *let (him) make.*
လုပ်ကြစို့ lohk-kyăh-zoh, *let us make.*
လုပ်ပါတော့ lohk pāh-daw, *please make (it).*

A FEW COMMON AUXILIARY VERBS.

ငါလုပ်ချင်သည် gnāh lohk chin-*thĕĕ*, *I wish to make.*

ငါလုပ်သင့်သည် gnāh lohk thin-*thĕĕ*, *I ought to make.*

ငါလုပ်တတ်သည် gnāh lohk tăht-thĕĕ, *I am wont to make.*

ငါလုပ်ဝံ့သည် gnāh lohk wŏŏn-*thĕĕ*, *I dare make.*

ငါလုပ်ရသည် gnā*h* lo*h*k yă*h-thëë*, ***I must make.***
ငါစလုပ်သည် gnā*h* tsă*h* lo*h*k thëë, ***I begin to make.***
ငါလုပ်နေသည် gnā*h* lo*h*k nay-*thëë*, ***I am making.***
ငါလုပ်စေသည် gnā*h* lo*h*k tsay-*thëë*, ***I cause to make.***
ငါလုပ်ခဲသည် gnā*h* lo*h*k hkeh-*thëë*, ***I seldom make.***
ငါလုပ်လိုသည် gnā*h* lo*h*k lo*h-thëë*, ***I wish to make.***
ငါလုပ်စမ်းမည် gnā*h* lo*h*k tsă*h*n:-mëë, ***I will try to make.***
ငါလုပ်ရာသည် gnā*h* lo*h*k yā*h-thëë*, ***I shou'd make.***
ငါလုပ်ပြန်မည် gnā*h* lo*h*k pyă*h*n-mëë, ***I will re-make.***
သေကုန်ပြီ thay ko*h*n-byee, ***(They) are quite dead.***
သေထိုက်သည် thay dik-thëë, ***(He) is worthy to die.***
ပြုလွယ်သည် pyŏŏ lweh-*thëë*, ***(It) is easy to do.***

NOTE.—In the above ငါ gnā*h* has been used for *I* for the sake of brevity.

THE CONSTRUCTION OF BURMESE SENTENCES.

1. The principal verb is always at the end of a sentence but followed by the modifying verb and the closing affix, if any; thus,

သူ	ထမင်း	စားသည်	
He	rice	eats	
ငါ	ထမင်း	စား	နိုင်သည်
I	rice	eat	can

2. If there is an adverb of time it must commence the sentence; thus,

မနေ့က	ငါ	မြို့သို့	သွားခဲ့ပြီ
Yesterday	I	town-to	went

3. After the adverbs of time another clause may be introduced; thus,

နက်ဖန်၊	ကျွန်ုပ်	အား	လျှင်၊	သင့်	အိမ်	ကို	လာ	မည်
To-morrow	I,	at leisure	if,	thy	house	to	come	will

4. The following is a typical sentence:—

ထို	အခါ	၌၊	ကောင်း	သော	လူ	နှစ်	ယောက်တို့	သည်
That	time	at,	good	[1]	man	two	[2]	

မြို့သို့	သွား	ကြ	လတ်	သော်	ရေ	တွင်းထဲသို့	လဲ
town-to	go	[3] happen	[4] having	[5] water (of)	hole	into	fall over

ကျ၍	သေခဲ့ လေ ၏
dropping[6]	died

Illustration of the Construction and Pronunciation of Burmese.

ထိုအခါ။ ဒုန္ဒိပိဋ္ဌအမည်ရှိ သောရွာ၌နေ သောဂူစကာအမည် ရှိသော ပုဏ္ဏားသည်၊ အလှူကိုလှည့်လည်ခံသဖြင့်၊ အသပြာတရာရ၏။ ထိုအသပြာတရာကို၊ မိမိမဆောင်နိုင်၊ အလိုလည်းမတိုင်သေးသောကြောင့်၊ ရွာတရွာတွင်တယောက် သောပုဏ္ဏားအိမ်၌ အပ်ထား၍၊ တဖန်အလှူခံသောအံ့ငှါ၊ အရပ်တပါးသို့လှည့်လည်သွားပြန်၏။

ထိုဂူစကာပုဏ္ဏားသည် အလှူခံသွား၍၊ တပါးအရပ်၌၊ နှစ်၊ လ၊ အရှည်ကြာမြင့်လေသော်၊ ဂူစကာပုဏ္ဏား၏ဥစ္စာကို သိမ်း၍၊ ထားသောပုဏ္ဏားသည်၊ သုံးစားနှင့်၍ကုန်လေ၏။

[1] Instead of ကောင်းသောလူ one might put လူကောင်း (see p. 113).

[2] ယောက် numeral affix (p. 80). တို့ plural affix (p. 109).

[3] ကြ plural affix for verbs (p. 115). [4] လတ် euphonic verbal affix (p. 120), gives an idea of unexpected suddenness.

[5] သော် past continuative affix (p. 119). [6] ၍ continuative affix (p. 119).

[7] ခဲ့ လေ ၏ past closing affixes (p. 121).

Phonetic Pronunciation and Literal Translation.[1]

Htoh ăh-hkāh, Dohnnĕewĕĕhtăh yŏŏāh-hnik nay-thaw
That time, Dohnnĕĕwĕĕhtăh village-in dwelling

Zoozăhgāh ăh-mĕĕ shĕĕ-thaw Pohnnāh:-thĕĕ, ăh-hloo-goh
Zoozăhgāh name having Brahman, alms

hleh̥-leh hkăhn - thăh-hpyin̥, ăhthăhbyāh tăh-yāh yăh-ĕĕ.
going about receive by (means of), coins 100 got.

Htoh ăhthăhbyāh tăh-yāh-goh, mĕĕ-mĕĕ măh sowng hning,
Those coins 100 self not carry able,

ăh-loh lee: măh ting thay: thaw̥-jowng̥, yŏŏāh tăh-hkŏŏ
desire also not attain(ed) yet because, village one-

dwin, tăh-yowk-thaw Pohnnāh: ayn - hnik ăht - htāh:-yŏŏay̥,
in, one (a) Brahman's house at give - put - ting,

tăh-hpăhn ăh-hloo hkăhn - thaw-ăhn̥-hgnāh, ăh-yăht tăh-bāh:-
again alms receive in order to (for), place other

thoh̥ hleh̥-leh thwāh:-byăhn-ĕĕ. Htoh Zoozăhgāh
to going-about went again. That Zoozăhgāh

Pohnnāh: - thĕĕ, ăh-hloo thwāh: hkăhn-yŏŏay̥, tăh-bāh:
Pohnnāh: alms go receiv - ing, other

ăh-yăht-hnik, hnit - lăh ăh-sheh kyāh-myin̥[2] - lay - thăw,
place - at, years-months long long - tall (having been),

ohksăh-goh thayn:-yŏŏay̥ htāh:-thaw - Pohnnāh: - thĕĕ,
the money taking charge of keeping Brahman (nom.),

thôhn:-zāh:-hnin̥-yŏŏay̥ kohn-lay-ĕĕ.
use - eat [3] had consumed.

[1] For Idiomatic Translation, see over.

[2] Myin̥ is lit. '*tall*,' but is often coupled with kyāh, '*long in time*.'

[3] နှင့် hnin̥, prior past tense affix.

[*Idiomatic Translation.*—At that time, a Brahman[1] named Zoozăhgāh, who dwelt in a village named Dohnnéewĕehtăh, by going about and receiving alms, amassed one hundred pieces (of silver). Not being able himself to carry those pieces, and because his desires were not yet satisfied, leaving them at the house of another Brahman in a certain village, he again wandered about to other places in order to receive alms once more.

That Zoozăhgāh, the Brahman, having been for months and years begging alms in other places, the Brahman who had taken charge of Zoozăhgāh the Brahman's wealth, had (before he, Z., returned) made away with and used it all up.]

POLITE MODES OF ADDRESS.

When one addresses a Burman it is rude to use the ordinary pronoun. If his position in society is known he should be addressed by the term that denotes his position, if not, one must generally suppose him or her to be 'the supporter of a monastery', ကျောင်းတကာ Kyowng:-tăhgāh (fem. ကျောင်းအမ Kyowng:-ăh-măh), or 'founder of a Pagoda', ဘုရားတကာ Hpăhyāh:-tăhgāh, or simply as ခင်ဗျား or ခင်ဗြား Hkin-byāh: (a short form of သခင်ဘုရား Master, object of reverence). If the person addressed is a teacher or person of learning, he should be called ဆရာ Săhyāh. In talking to a priest or teacher, instead of saying 'I', one should use တပည့်တော် Tăhbeh-dāw (scholar), and call him ကိုယ်တော် Kō-dāw, or ဆရာတော် Săhyāh-dāw. To a person in authority a Burman would always designate himself as ကျွန်တော် Kyōōn-dāw (Royal servant), but an Englishman would say 'Kyōōnohk'.

ကတော် Kăhdāw means *lady* and is used for the wives of honourable persons, as မင်းကတော် Min: kăhdāw, ဆရာကတော် Săhyāh kăhdāw, for the wives of magistrates and teachers.

The word တကာ tăh-gāh, which is used above, is a corruption of the Pali word ဒါယကာ dāh-yăh-kāh, *a giver*; the feminine is တကာမ tăh-gāh-măh.

---

[1] The proper word for Brahman is *Byăhmăh*ṇăh, but the Burmese usually use the word ပုဏ္ဏား, Pohṇṇāh:, which is a word of doubtful derivation.

CONVERSATIONAL PHRASES AND SENTENCES.[1]

Useful and Necessary Idiomatic Expressions.

များစွာ အသုံးဝင်သောစကားဆက်များ။

English.	Burmese.	Pronunciation.
Thank you (seldom used)	ကျေးဇူးတင်ပါသည်	Kyay:-zoo: tin-bā*h*-*th*ëë
Yes	ဟုတ်ပါ။ ဟုတ်ကဲ့	Ho*h*k-pā*h* *or* ho*h*k-hkę*h*
No	မဟုတ်ဘူး။ မဟုတ်ပါ	Mă*h*-ho*h*k-hpoo:, mă*h*-ho*h*k-pā*h*
Bring	ယူခဲ့ပါ	Yoo-gę*h*-bā*h*
Bring that	ထိုသင်းကိုယူခဲ့ပါ	Ho*h*-din:-go*h* yoo-gę*h*-bā*h*
Give me	ကျွန်ုပ်ကိုပေးပါ	Kyŏŏno*h*k-ko*h* pay:-bā*h*
Give it him	သူ့ကိုပေးလိုက်ပါ	Thŏŏ-go*h* pay:-lik-pā*h*
Do (you) understand?	နားလည်သလား	Nā*h*: leh-*th*ă*h*-lā*h*:
(I) do not understand	နားမလည်ဘူး	Nā*h*: mă*h* leh-boo:
Send (it) to me	ကျွန်ုပ်ထံသို့ပို့လိုက်ပါ	Kyŏŏno*h*k htă*h*n-*th*o*h* po*h*-lik-pā*h*
Tell me	ကျွန်ုပ်ကိုပြောပါ	Kyŏŏno*h*k-ko*h* pyaw-bā*h*
Tell him	သူ့ကိုပြောလိုက်ပါ	Thŏŏ-go*h* pyaw-lik-pā*h*
Can you tell (me)?	ပြောနိုင်ပါမည်လား	Pyaw ning-bā*h*-mëë-lā*h*:
Can you speak English?	အင်္ဂလိပ်စကားတတ်သလား	Ingă*h*layk tsa*h*-gā*h*: tă*h*t-thă*h*-lā*h*:

[1] See 'Hints on addressing a Burman', p. 24; 'Polite Modes of Address', p. 126.

English.	Burmese.	Pronunciation.
Is there any one here who speaks English?	အင်္ဂလိပ်စကားတတ် သောသူရှိသလား	Ingā*h*layk tsă*h* -gā*h*: tă*h*t-thaw-thoo shēē-*th*ă*h*-lāh:
What do (you) say?	ဘာပြောသလဲ။ ဘာ ဆိုသလဲ	Bā*h* pyaw-*th*ă*h*-leh, Bā*h* so*h*-*th*ă*h*-leh
Ask him (inquire)	သူကိုမေးစမ်းပါ	Thŏŏ-go*h* may:-ză*h*n:-
Ask for (demand	တောင်းပါတော့	Towng:-bā*h*-daw̥ [bā*h*
Speak loudly [it)	ကျယ်ကျယ်ပြောပါ	Kyeh-jeh pyaw-bā*h*
Never mind	အတွက်မရှိပါဘူး	Ă*h*-twet mă*h* shēē-bā*h*-bo̥o:
What is to be done?	ဘာပြုသင့်သလဲ	Bā*h* pyŏŏ *th*in̥-*th*ă*h*-leh
Why?	ဘာပြုလို့လဲ	Bā*h* pyŏŏ-lo̥*h* leh
What is it? [ter?	ဘာလဲ	Bā*h* leh
What is the mat-	ဘာဖြစ်သလဲ	Bā*h* hpyit-thă*h*-leh
Do (you) hear?	ကြားသလား	Kyā*h*:-*th*ă*h*-lā*h*:
I understand, Sir	နားလည်သည်၊ ဘုရား	Nā*h*: leh-*th*ēē, hpă*h*yā*h*:
Carry this	သည်ဟာကိုထမ်းပါ	*Th*ēē hā*h*-go*h* htă*h*n:-bā*h* [daw̥
Take that	ထိုဟာကိုယူပါတော့	Hto*h* hā*h*-go*h* yoo-bā*h*-
Take (it) away	ယူသွားလိုက်	Yoo-thwā*h*:-lik
Make haste!	အလျင်ပြုပါ	A*h*-lyin pyŏŏ-bā*h*
Come quickly	မြန်မြန်လာခဲ့	Myă*h*n-myă*h*n lā*h*-geh̥
Take care!	သတိပြုပါ	Thă*h*dēē pyŏŏ-bā*h*
Listen!	နားထောင်ပါ	Nā*h*: htowng-bā*h*
Come in!	ဝင်ပါတော့	Win-bā*h*-daw̥
Come here!	သည်ကိုလာခဲ့	Dee-go*h* lā*h*-geh̥
Come back!	ပြန်လာခဲ့	Pyă*h*n lā*h*-geh̥
Call my servant (boy)	ကျွန်ုပ်လူကလေးကို ခေါ်ပါ	Kyŏŏno*h*k loogă*h*lay:-go*h* hkāw-bă*h*

English.	Burmese.	Pronunciation.
Take this note to —	သည်စာကို — ထံသို့ ယူသွားပါ	*Th*ee tsā*h*-go*h*—htă*h*n-*th*oh̥ yoo-thwā*h*:-bā*h*
Bring back an answer	ပြန်စာကိုယူခဲ့	Pyă*h*n-zā*h*-go*h* yoo-geh̥
Stand still a moment	ခဏရပ်နေပါဦး	Hkă*h*nă*h* yă*h*t-nay-bā*h*-ô*h*n:
Go away (rough)	သွားလိုက်	Thwā*h*:-lik
Go away (polite)	သွားပါတော့	Thwā*h*:-bā*h*-daw̥
Good-bye[1]	သွားဦးတော့	Thwā*h*:-ô*h*n:-daw̥
Too soon	ဦးလွန်းသည်။ စောလွန်းသည်	Oo:-loon:-*th*ĕĕ, tsaw-loon:-*th*ĕĕ
Too late	နောက်ကျလွန်းသည်	Nowk-kyă*h* loon: *th*ëë:
Very well (good)	ကောင်းပါပြီ	Kowng:-bā*h*-byee
What do you want?	ဘာလိုချင်သလဲ	Bā*h* lo*h*-jin-thă*h*-leh
How do you do? / Are you well?	မာပါ၏လား	Mā*h*-bā*h*-ëë-lā*h*:
I am well	မာပါ၏	Mā*h*-bā*h*-ëë
Much obliged	ကျေးဇူးကြီးလှပြီ	Kyay:zoo̥: kee:-hlă*h*-byee
There is nothing	ဘာမျှမရှိဘူး	Bā*h*-hmyă*h* mă*h* shëë-[boo:
Nothing is the matter	ဘာမျှမဖြစ်ဘူး	Bā*h*-hmyă*h* mă*h* hpyit-hpoo:
No trouble at all	နှောင့်ရှက်စရာမရှိ	Hno̥wng-shet-tsă*h*-yā*h* mă*h* shëë
Who is there?	ထိုမှာဘယ်သူရှိသလဲ	Ho*h*-hmā*h* beh-*th*oo sheë-*th*ă*h*-leh

[1] The person who pays a call on leaving says သွားတော့မည်နော် thwā*h*:-daw-mĕĕ-nāw, *I will go?* and the person in the house replies သွားဦးတော့ thwā*h*:-ô*h*n:daw, *Go and return.*

English.	Burmese.	Pronunciation.
It is I	ကျွန်ုပ်ပါ။ ကျွန်တော်ပါ	Kyŏŏno*h*k-pā*h*, kyŏŏn-dāw-bā*h* [leh
What is the news?	ဘယ်သိတင်းရသလဲ	Beh thă*h*din: yă*h*-thă*h*-
There is no news	ဘယ်သိတင်းမျှမရ	Beh thă*h*din: hmyă*h* mă*h* yă*h*
Do you know for certain?	ဧကန်အမှန်သိသလား	Aykă*h*n ă*h*-hmă*h*n theē-*thăh*-lā*h*: [daw
Go in front	အရှေ့သို့သွားတော့	Ă*h*-shay-*thoh*-thwā*h*:
Follow	နောက်သို့လိုက်ပါ	Nowk-tho*h* lik-pā*h*
Go home	အိမ်သို့သွားတော့	Ayn-*thŏh* thwā*h*:-daw
Go to the post office and ask for my letters	စာတိုက်သို့သွား၍ ကျွန်ုပ်စာများကို တောင်းပါ	Tsā*h*-dik-tho*h* thwā*h*:-yooay kyŏŏno*h*k tsā*h*-myā*h*:-go*h* towng:-bā*h* [zo*h*
Let us start	ထွက်သွားကြစို့	Htwet-thwā*h*:-jă*h*-
Wait	နေပါဦး။ စောင့်ပါ	Nay-bā*h*-ō*h*n:, tsowng bā*h*:
Bring my horse	ကျွန်ုပ်မြင်းကိုယူခဲ့	Kyŏŏno*h*k myin:-go*h* yoo-geh
Saddle it	ခုန်းနှီးတင်ပါ	Hko*h*n:-hnee: tin-bā*h*
Call the interpreter [man say?	စကားပြန်ကိုခေါ်ပါ	Tsă*h*-gă*h*-byă*h*n-go*h* hkāw bā*h* [*thăh*-leh
What does that	ဟိုလူဘာပြောသလဲ	Ho*h* loo bā*h* pyaw-
He says he cannot find the horse	မြင်းကိုမတွေ့နိုင်ဘူး တည့်	Myin:-go*h* mă*h* tway hning boo:, deh
He thinks some one has stolen it	တစုံတယောက်ခိုးယူ သည်ဟုထင်သည်	Tă*h*-zo*h*n-tă*h*-yowk-hko*h* yoo-thă*h*-lo*h* htin-*th*eē [lā*h*:
Is it possible?	ဖြစ်နိုင်ပါမည်လား	Hpyit-hning-bā*h*-meē

English.	Burmese.	Pronunciation.
It is his fault	သူအပြစ်ပေ	Thŏŏ ă*h*-pyit pay
He is sorry	သူဝမ်းနည်းပါသည်	Thoo woon:-neh:-bā*h*-*th*ëë
He must get me another horse	သူကျွန်နုပ်ဘို့မြင်းတကောင်ရှာပေးရမည်	Thoo kyŏŏnohk-hpo̥*h* myin: tă*h*-gowng shā*h*-pay:-yă*h*-mëë
Who is paddling that boat?	ဟိုလှေကိုဘယ်သူလှော်သလဲ	Ho*h* hlay-go*h* beh*th*oo hlăw-*th*ă*h*-leh
Is it a man or a woman?	ယောကျ်ားလား၊ မိန္မလား	Yowkyā*h*: lā*h*:, mayn:-mă*h* lā*h*:
It is a woman	မိန္မပေ	Mayn:mă*h* bay
It is a woman [1]	မိန္မပေါ့	Mayn:mă*h* baw̥
Well done!	ကောင်းပေ	Kowng: bay
How fortunate	တယ်ကံကောင်းသဥ်	Teh kă*h*n kowng:-*th*ëë
It is a fact	သည်ဟာအမှန်ပေ	Thee hā*h* ă*h*-hmă*h*n bay [hnin̥
Don't be angry	စိတ်မဆိုးပါနှင့်	Tsayt-mă*h*-sô*h*:-bā*h*-
How beautiful	တယ်လှသဥ်ကို	Teh hlă*h*-*th*ëë, go*h*
Be silent!	တိတ်တိတ်နေ	Tayt-tayt nay
Long ago	ကြာလှပြီ [သည်	Kyā*h* hlă*h* byee [*th*ëë
Shameful	ရှက်စရာကောင်း	Shet-tsă*h*-yā*h* kowng:-
Are you not ashamed?	မရှက်ဘူးလား	Mă*h* shet-hpoo:-lā*h*:
(You) are to blame	အပြစ်တင်စရာကောင်းသည်	Ă*h*-pyit-tin-ză*h*-yā*h* kowng:-*th*ëë
Get up!	ထလိုက်။ (polite) ထပါ	Htă*h*-lik, htă*h*-bā*h*

[1] I. e. how could you think otherwise?

Meals. ထမင်းစားကြောင်း။

(For Vocabularies, see pp. 49-53.)

English.	Burmese.	Pronunciation.
Breakfast (dinner, or supper) is ready	ထမင်းပျှင်းပြီးပြီ	Htă*h*min: pyin-pyee:-byee
Is the tea made ?	လက်ဖက်ရည်လုပ်ပြီးပြီလား	Lă*h*-hpet-yĕĕ lo*h*k-pyee:-byee-lā*h*:
Do you drink coffee ?	ကာဖီရည်သောက်တတ်သလား	Kā*h*-hpee-yĕĕ thowk tă*h*t-thă*h*-lā*h*: [*th*ĕĕ
This milk is sour	သည်နို့ရည်ချဉ်သည်	*Th*ee no*h*-yĕĕ chin-
Bring me an egg	ကြက်ဥတလုံးယူခဲ့	Kyet-ŏŏ tă*h*-lô*h*n: yoo-geh
Must I boil the egg ?	ကြက်ဥကိုပြုတ်ရမည်လား	Kyet-ŏŏ-go*h* pyo*h*k-yă*h*-mĕĕ-lā*h*:
Fry me two eggs	ကြက်ဥနှစ်လုံးကြော်ပေးပါ	Kyet-ŏŏ hnă*h*-lô*h*n: kyāw-pay:-bā*h*
This butter is rancid [butter	သည်ထောပတ်ဟောင်စပ်သည်	*Th*ee htāwbă*h*t howng-ză*h*t-*th*ĕĕ [ô*h*n:
Bring some other	ထောပတ်ယူခဲ့ဦး	Htawbă*h*t yoo-geh-
We want more tea-cups	လက်ဖက်ရည်ပုကန်များလိုသေးသည်	Lă*h*-hpet-yĕĕ-pă*h*gă*h*n-myā*h*: lo*h*-*th*ay:-*th*ĕĕ
Remove the dishes	ပုကန်ပြားများကိုယူသွားတော့	Pă*h*gă*h*n-byā*h*:-myā*h*:-go*h* yoo-thwā*h*:-daw
Cook some pork curry for dinner	ညစာတို့ဝက်သားဟင်းချက်ပေးပါ	Nyă*h*-zā*h*-bo*h* wet-thā*h*: hin: chet-pay:-bā*h*

English.	Burmese.	Pronunciation.
Take care to boil the rice well, too	ထမင်းကိုလည်း ကောင်းကောင်း နပ်အောင်သတိပြု လိုက်	Htă*h*min:-go*h* lee: kowng:-gowng: nă*h*t-owng thă*h*deë pyŏŏ lik
Change the plates	ပုကန်များကိုလဲလိုက် ပါ	Pă*h*gă*h*n-myā*h*:-go*h* leh-lik-pā*h*
Give me a clean knife and fork	စားပွဲဓါးနှင့်ခက်ရင်း အသစ်ကိုယူခဲ့	Tsā*h*-bweh-dā*h*:-hnin hkă*h*-yin: ă*h*-thit-ko*h* yoo-geh
Give me a glass of water	ရေတခွက်ပေးပါ	Yay tă*h*-hkwet pay:-bā*h*
Pour out the tea	လက်ဖက်ရည်ကိုငှဲ့ ပေးပါ	Lă*h*-hpet-yee-go*h* hngeh pay:-bā*h*
How many are coming to dinner?	ဘယ်နှစ်ယောက်ထ မင်းစားလာမည်လဲ	Beh-hnă*h*-yowk htă*h*-min: tsā*h*:-lā*h*-mëë-leh
I think there will be eight persons	လူရှစ်ယောက်လာ မည်လို့ထင်ပါသည်	Loo-shit-yowk lā*h*-mëë-lo*h* htin-bā*h*-*th*ëë

Health. ကျန်းမာခြင်းနှင့်ဆိုင်သောအကြောင်း။

(For Vocabulary, see p. 47.)

Are you well?	မာ၏လား	Mā*h*-ëë-lā*h*:
I am well	မာပါ၏	Mā*h*-bā*h*-ëë
I am very ill	အလွန်နာပါသည်	Ă*h*-lŏŏn nā*h*-bā*h*-*th*ëë
I am not very well	ကောင်းကောင်းမ မာဘူး	Kowng:-gowng: mă*h* mā*h*-boo:

English.	Burmese.	Pronunciation.
I hope you will soon be better.	ခင်ဗြားမြန်မြန်ကျမ်းမာရန်ကျွန်တော်မျှော်လင့်ပါသည်	Hkinbyā*h*: myă*h*n-myă*h*n kyă*h*n:-mā*h*-yă*h*n kyŏŏn-dāw hmyāw-lin-bā*h*-*th*ĕĕ
Do you sleep well?	အအိပ်ကောင်းသလား	Ă*h*-ayk kowng:-*th*ă*h*-lā*h*:
I sleep pretty well	တော်တော်ကောင်းကောင်းအိပ်ပါသည်	Tāw-dāw kowng:-gowng: ayk-pā*h*-*th*ĕĕ [*th*ĕĕ
I have caught a cold	နှာစေးနာရှိသည်	Hnā*h*-zee:-nā*h* shĕĕ-
I feel sick	အန်ချင်သည်	Ă*h*n jin-*th*ĕĕ
Send for a doctor	ဆေးသမားကိုခေါ်လိုက်	Say:thă*h*mā*h*:-go*h* hkāw-lik
I want to see a doctor	ဆေးသမားနှင့်တွေ့ချင်သည်	Say:thă*h*mā*h*:-hnin tway-jin-*th*ĕĕ
She (*or* he) has a cough	သူမှာချောင်းဆိုးနာရှိသည်	Thoo-hmā*h* chowng:-zo*h*:-nā*h* shĕĕ-*th*ĕĕ
Where is the chemist's shop?	ဆေးဆိုင်ဘယ်မှာလဲ	Say:-zing beh-hmā*h*-leh
How far is it from here?	သည်ကဘယ်လောက်ဝေးသလဲ	Dee-gă*h* beh-lowk way:-*th*ă*h*-leh
You must drink this	သည်ဟာကိုသောက်ရမည်	Dee hā*h*-go*h* thowk-yă*h*-mĕĕ
Have you any brandy (spirit)?	ဗြန်ဒီအရက်ရှိသလား	Byă*h*ndee-ă*h*-yet shĕĕ-*th*ă*h*-lā*h*:
I can eat nothing	ဘာမျှမစားနိုင်ဘူး	Bā*h*-hmyă*h* mă*h* tsā*h*: hning-boo:
I can swallow nothing	တစုံတခုမျှမမြိုနိုင်ဘူး	Tă*h*-zo*h*n tă*h*-hkŏŏ-hmyă*h* mă*h* myo*h* hning-boo:

English.	Burmese.	Pronunciation.
My head aches	ကျွန်ုပ်ခေါင်းကိုက်သည်	Kyŏŏnoh*k* gowng: kik-thëë
My foot is swollen	ကျွန်ုပ်ခြေရောင်နေသည်	Kyŏŏnoh*k* chee yowng-nay-*th*ëë
I cannot get up	မထနိုင်ပါဘူး	Mă*h* htă*h* hning-bā*h*-boo:
May I get up ?	ထချင်လျှင်ထနိုင်ပါသလား	Htă*h*-jin-hlyin htă*h*-hning-bā*h*-*th*ah-lā*h*:
Give me a cup of tea	လက်ဖက်ရည်တခွက်ပေးပါ	Lă*h*-hpet-yëë tă*h*-hkwet pay:-bā*h*
I have been ill three days	နာနေတာသုံးရက်ရှိပြီ	Nā*h*-nay-[1]dā*h* thô*h*n: yet shĕë-byee
Give me a bit of bread	မုန့်တစိတ်ပေးပါ	Mo*h*n tă*h*-zayt pay:-bā*h*
I must wash my hands	ကျွန်ုပ်လက်ဆေးရမည်	Kyŏŏnoh*k* let say:-yă*h*-mëë
I have washed my face	မျက်နှာကိုသစ်ခဲ့ပြီ	Myet-hnā*h*-go*h* thit-hkeh-byee
There is no soap	ဆပ်ပြာမရှိ	Să*h*tpyā*h* mă*h*-shĕë
It is not good to go out when it is cold	ချမ်းသောအခါ၌အပြင်သို့သွားသို့မကောင်းဘူး	Chă*h*n:-*th*aw ă*h*-hkā*h*-hnik ă*h*-pyin-*th*o*h* thwā*h*:-bo*h*-mă*h* kowng:-boo:

[1] The တာ dā*h* is a contraction of သည် *thëë* (the verb affix) and ဟာ hā*h*, *a thing*, which is often used in colloquial and might be translated '*the fact of being ill has been three days*'.

Time. အချိန်။ အခါ။ ကာလ။

(For Vocabulary, see p. 36.)

English.	Burmese.	Pronunciation.
What time is it?	ဘယ်နှစ်နာရီလောက်ရှိသလဲ။ ဘယ်အချိန်ရှိသလဲ	Beh-hnăh năhyee lowk shëë-*thăh*-leh, *or* Beh ăh-chayn shëë-*thăh*-leh
Ten minutes past seven	ခုနှစ်နာရီနှင့်ခုနှစ်မိနစ်လောက်ရှိသည်	Hkŏŏ-hnăh năhyee-hnin̥ hkŏŏ-hnăh mëënit-lowk shëë-*th*ëë
It has just struck nine	ယခုဘဲကိုးနာရီထိုးပြီ	Yăh-hkŏŏ-beh kôh:-năhyee htee:-byee
The clock is striking	နာရီယခုထိုးနေသည်	Năhyee yăh-hkŏŏ htee: nay-*th*ëë
A quarter past one (afternoon)	မွန်းလွဲတနာရီနှင့်တဆိတ်	Mŏŏn:-lweh: tăh-năh-yee-hnin̥ tăh-zayt
Half-past four (morning)	မနက်လေးနာရီခွဲ	Măhnet lay:-năhyee gweh
A quarter to eight	ရှစ်နာရီမတ်တင်း	Shit-năhyee măht tin:
At what time?	ဘယ်အချိန်မှာလဲ	Beh ăh-chayn-hmăh leh
It is noon	မွန်းတည့်အချိန်ဖြစ်သည်	Mŏŏn:-deh̥ ăh-chayn hpyit-thëë
Wake me at midnight	သန်းခေါင်ကျွန်ုပ်ကိုနှိုးပါ	Thăh-gowng kyŏŏn-ohk-koh hnôh:-băh
I will get up at six in the morning	မနက်ခြောက်နာရီမှာထပါမည်	Măhnetchowk-năhyee-hmăh htăh-băh-mëë

English.	Burmese.	Pronunciation.
He will arrive at half-past five in the evening	ညနေငါးနာရီခွဲ လောက်သူရောက် ပါလိမ့်မည်	Nyăh-nay gnāh:-năh-yee-gweh lowk thoo yowk-pāh-laym-mĕĕ
I shall dine exactly at seven in the evening	ညနေ့ခုနှစ်နာရီတိတိ ကျွန်ုပ်ထမင်းစား မည်	Nyăh-nay hkŏŏ-hnăh-nāhyee htĕĕ-hdĕĕ kyŏŏnohk htăhmin: tsāh:-mĕĕ
What month is it?	သည်လဘယ်လလဲ	Thee lăh beh lăh leh
What day (of the week) is to-day?	သည်ကနေ့ဘာနေ့ဘဲ	Thigah-nay bah nay leh
What day of the month is this?	သည်ကနေ့ဘယ်နှစ် ရက်နေ့လဲ	Thigăh-nay beh-hnăh yet-nay leh

NOTE.—The Burmese date is 638 years after the Christian era. Therefore, in order to get the Burmese year, we have to subtract that number from our year. Both eras are used, and, to distinguish the one from the other, the word သက္ကရာဇ် Thekkăh-yit is placed before the Burmese date; thus, သက္ကရာဇ် ၁၂၇၂ = A. D. 1910. Both Burmese and English months are used, and often the two together, in documents.

The month is divided into two parts, လဆန်း lăh-zăhn:, *the waxing*, and လပြည့်ကျော် lăh-byĕĕ-jāw or လဆုတ် lăh-zohk, *the waning*. The full moon, လပြည့် lăh-byĕĕ, falls on the fifteenth of the waxing; the လကွယ် lăh-gweh (*hidden moon*) falls on the fourteenth or fifteenth of the wane. The days of worship are the full moon, eighth of the wane, the hidden moon, and the eighth waxing; otherwise the days of the week are not observed, though noted. (The Englishman observes Sunday, the Burman does not.)

Times, Seasons, and Weather.

ဥတု၊အချိန်များနှင့်မိုးလေအကြောင်း။

(For Vocabulary, see p. 36.)

English.	Burmese.	Pronunciation.
This day week	သည်နေ့ကခုနှစ်ရက်နေ့	*Th*ee nay-gă*h* hkŏŏ-hnă*h*-yet nay
That was three or four days ago	သုံးလေးရက်လောက်ရှိပြီ	Thô*h*n: lay:-yet lowk sheē-byee
To-morrow fortnight	နက်ဖန်နေ့နောက်ဆယ်လေးရက်	Net-hpă*h*n-nay nowk seh-lay:-yet
At about this time	ယခုအချိန်လောက်မှာ	Yă*h*-hkŏŏ ă*h*-chayn-lowk-hmā*h*
In a month's time	ယခုနေ့ကတလလောက်	Yă*h*-hkŏŏ-nay-gă*h* tă*h*-lă*h* lowk
The first of next month	ယခုလာမည့်လထရက်နေ့	Yă*h*-hkŏŏ lā*h*-mēĕ-lă*h* tă*h*-yet nay
In (after) six weeks	ယနေ့ကတလနှင့်ဆယ်လေးရက်	Yă*h*-nay-gă*h* tă*h*-lă*h*-hnin seh-lay:-yet
On the last day of the month	ယခုထကွယ်နေ့	Yā*h*-hkŏŏ lă*h*-gweh-nay
At the end of this month	သည်လကုန်မှာ	*Th*ee lá*h* go*h*n hmā*h*
Towards the middle of January	ဇနဝါရီထ၁၅ရက်နေ့ထောက်	Ză*h*nă*h*wā*h*yee lă*h* seh-gnā*h*:-yet nay lowk
In the course of a week	ခုနှစ်ရက်အတွင်းတွင်	Hkŏŏ-hnă*h*-yet ă*h*-twin:-dwin
From time to time	အဖန်ဖန်	Ă*h*-hpă*h*n-bă*h*n

English.	Burmese.	Pronunciation.
From one day to another	တနေ့ကတနေ့သို့	Tăh-nay-gah tăh-nay-thoh [thay:
A few days ago	နေ့ရက်မကြာသေး	Nay-yet măh kyāh
A short time since [ago	ကာလမရှည်ပြီ	Kăhlăh măh shay-byee [thay:
Scarcely two days	နှစ်ရက်မရှိသေး	Hnăh-yet măh shëë
A month ago	တလရှိပြီ	Táh-lăh shëë-byee
It is full moon	လပြည့်နေ့ဖြစ်သည်	Lăh-byëë-nay hpyit-
Last year [last	မနှစ်က	Măh-hnit-kăh [thëë
The year before	တမျန်နှစ်	Tăh-myăhn-hnit
It is not long since	မကြာသေးဘူး	Măh kyāh thay: boo:
Long ago	ကြာလှပြီ	Kyāh-hlăh-byee
Once in (three) days	(သုံး) ရက်တခါ	(Thohn:) yet tăh-hkāh
The heat of the sun is unbearable	နေပူလို့မခံနိုင်ဘူး	Nay poo loh măh hkăhn-hning-boo:
I am very warm	တယ်အိုက်သည်	Teh ik-thëë
I am afraid it will rain	မိုးယ်းရွာမည့်စိုးသည်	Môh: yŏŏāh-mëë, tsôh:-thëë
Did you see the lightning?	လျှတ်စစ်ကိုမြင်သလား	Shăht-tsit-koh myin-thăh-lāh:
I heard the thunder	မိုယ်းခြိမ်းသံကိုကြားခဲ့သည်	Môh:chôhn:-thăhn-goh kyāh: geh thëë
How it pours!	တယ်မိုးယ်းရွာသည်	Teh môh: yŏŏāh-thëë
Would you like an umbrella?	ထီးလိုချင်သလား	Htee: loh-jin-thăh-lāh: [tsoh-byee
I am wet through	အဝတ်များစွတ်စိုပြီ	Ăh-wŏŏt-myāh: tsŏŏt-
Look at the rainbow	သက်တံကိုကြည့်လိုက်ပါ	Thettăhn-goh kyëë-lik-pāh

English.	Burmese.	Pronunciation.
It is growing very cold	တယ်အေးလာသဉ်	Teh ay: lā*h*-*th*ěě
It is very dirty	တယ်ရှုံများသည်	Teh shŏŏn myā*h*:-*th*ěě
It is very windy	တယ်လေတိုက်သည်	Teh lay tik-thěě
The wind is in the east	လေအရှေ့ဖက်က လာသည်	Lay ă*h*-shay bekkă*h* lā*h*-*th*ëë
The dust is terrible	တယ်ဖုံထသည်	Teh hpo*h*n htă*h*-*th*ěě
How bright the moon is	တယ်လသာသည်	Teh lă*h* thā*h*-*th*ëë
The sky is overcast, so I think it will rain	မိုယ်းအုံ့လို့မိုယ်းရွာ မည်လို့ထင်သည်	Mô*h*: o*h*n-lo*h* mô*h*: yŏŏā*h*-mëë-lo*h*, htin-*th*ëë
The stars are bright	ကြယ်များအလွှန်ထွန်း လင်းသည်	Kyeh-myā*h*: ă*h*-hlŏŏn htoon:-lin:-*th*eë
It will be fine to-morrow, I think	နက်ဖန်နေသာမည် ထင်သည်	Net-hpă*h*n nay thā*h*-mëĕ, htin-*th*ëë

Correspondence, Post, Telegraph, and Telephone.

စာရေးကြောင်းနှင့်စာတိုက်၊ ကြေးနန်းရုံးအကြောင်းများ။

(For Vocabulary, see p. 70.)

Have any letters come this morning?	ယခုမနက်စာများ ရောက်ပြီလား	Yă*h*-hkŏŏ mă*h*-net tsā*h*-myā*h*: yowk-pyee-lā*h*:
No, none have come yet	မလာမရောက်သေး ဘူး	Mă*h* lā*h* mă*h* yowk *th*ay: boo:
He ought to be here by now	သူယခုသည်ကို ရောက်သင့်ပြီ	Thoo yă*h*-hkŏŏ dee-go*h* yowk-thin-byee

English.	Burmese.	Pronunciation.
I have heard nothing	တစုံတခုမျှမကြားရသေးဘူး	Tă*h*-zo*h*n tă*h*-hkŏŏ hmyă*h* mă*h* kyā*h*:-yă*h*-*th*ay:-boo:
Has the mail steamer arrived?	စာပို့မီးသင်္ဘောရောက်ပြီလား	Tsā*h*-bo̥*h* mee:-thim:-baw yowk-pyee-lā*h*:
Go and see if the mail is in	ဒက်ရောက်သည်မရောက်သည်ကိုသွားကြည့်စမ်းပါ	Det yowk-thēē mă*h* yowk-thēē-go*h* thwā*h*: kye̥ē-ză*h*n: bā*h*
Are there any letters for me?	ကျွန်ုပ်ဘို့စာများရှိသလား	Kyŏŏno*h*k-hpo̥*h* tsā*h*-myā*h*: shĕĕ-*th*ă*h*-lā*h*:
I have not received any letter	စာတစောင်မျှမရဘူး	Tsā*h* tă*h*-zowng-hmyă*h* mă*h* yă*h*-boo:
Please post this letter	သည်စာကိုစာတိုက်သစ်တာထဲမှာထည့်လိုက်ပါ	*Th*ee tsā*h*-go*h* tsā*h*-dik thit-htā*h*-deh-hmā*h* hte̥h-lik-pā*h*
Please forward my letters to . . .	ကျွန်ုပ်စာများကိုပို့လိုက်ပါ	Kyŏŏno*h*k tsā*h*-myā*h*:-go*h* po̥*h*-lik-pā*h*
Please weigh this letter	သည်စာကိုချိန်စမ်းပါ	*Th*ee tsā*h*-go*h* chayn-ză*h*n:-bā*h*
I want some note-paper	စာရေးရန်စက္ကူလိုချင်သည်	Tsā*h*-yay:-yă*h*n tsek-koo lo*h*-jin-*th*ēē
Give me an envelope	စာအိပ်တခုပေးပါ	Tsā*h*-ayk tă*h*-hkŏŏ pay:-bā*h*
Where is the ink?	မှင်အိုးဘယ်မှာလဲ	Hmin-ô*h*: beh-hmā*h* leh
Lend me a piece of blotting-paper	မှင်နှိပ်စက္ကူတခြပ်ပေးပါ	Hmin-hnayk tsek-kŏŏ tă*h*-chă*h*t pay:-bā*h*

English.	Burmese.	Pronunciation.
Get me some stamps	တံဆိပ်ခေါင်းများပေးပါ	Tă*h*-zayt-gowng:-myā*h*: pay:-bā*h*
Tell him to wait	စောင့်နေလို့သူကိုပြောပါ	Tsowng nay-lo*h* thŏŏ-go*h* pyaw-bā*h*
I will send a reply later	နောက်မှပြန်စာပို့ပါမည်	Nowk-hmă*h* pyă*h*n-zā*h* po*h*-bā*h*-mĕĕ
Can I send a telegram?	ကြေးနန်းရိုက်နိုင်ပါမည်လား	Kyay:-na*h*n: yik hning-bā*h*-mĕĕ-lā*h*:
How much is the postage on these letters?	သည်စာများအတွက်စာပို့ခဘယ်လောက်ပေးရမည်လဲ	*Th*ee tsā*h*-myā*h*: ă*h*-twet tsā*h*-bo*h*-gă*h* beh-lowk pay:-yă*h*-mĕĕ-leh
I am just going to read it	ယခုဘဲဖတ်ပါမည်	Yă*h*-hkŏŏ-beh hpă*h*t-pā*h*-mĕĕ
Can you lend me a pencil?	ခဲတံတချောင်းခဏငှါးပါ	Hke*h*-dă*h*n tă*h*-chowng: hkă*h*nă*h* hgnā*h*:-bā*h*
What is your telephone number?	ခင်ဗျားနံပါတ်ဘယ်လောက်လဲ	Hken byā*h*: nă*h*mbă*ht* beh-lowk leh
My number is —	ကျွန်ုပ်နံပါတ်ဖြစ်ပါသည်	Kyŏŏno*h*k nă*h*mbă*h*t — hpyit-pā*h*-*th*ĕĕ
Put me through to —	— ကိုသွယ်ပေးပါ	— go*h* thweh-pay:-bā*h*
Line engaged	လမ်းမအားပါ	Lă*h*n: mă*h* ā*h*:-bā*h*
Ring up (Mr. Smith)[1]	မစ္စတာစမစ်ကိုစကားပြောသံကြိုးနှင့်ပြောပါ	(Mistā*h* Să*h*mit)-go*h* tsă*h*gā*h*:-pyaw-thă*h*n-jo*h*-hning pyaw-bā*h*

[1] This is translated 'Speak to Mr. Smith with the telephone.'

In Town. မြို့တွင်အကြောင်းအရာ။

English.	Burmese.	Pronunciation.
Where shall we go?	ကျွန်ုပ်တို့ဘယ်ကိုအလည်သွားမည်လဲ	Kyŏŏno*h*k-dọ*h* beh-go*h* ă*h*-leh-thwā*h*: mĕĕ-leh
Let us go to the post office	စာတိုက်သို့သွားကြစို့	Tsā*h*-dik-thọ*h* thwā*h*: jyă*h*-zọ*h*
Where does this road go?	သည်လမ်းဘယ်ရောက်သလဲ	*Th*ee lă*h*n: beh yowk-thă*h*-leh
Go up the street	လမ်းကိုလိုက်သွား	Lă*h*n:-go*h* lik-thwā*h*:
Is it far from here?	သည်ကကွာဝေးသလား	Dee-gă*h* kwā*h*-way:-*th*ă*h*-lā*h*:
Show me the way	လမ်းကိုပြပါ	Lă*h*n:-go*h* pyă*h*-bā*h*
Turn to the right	လက်ယာဘက်သို့လှည့်သွားလိုက်	Let-yā*h*-bet-thọ*h* hleh-thwā*h*:-lik
Turn to the left	လက်ဝဲဘက်သို့လှည့်	Let-weh-bet-thọ*h* hleh-thwā*h*:
Go straight on	ရှေ့သို့တည့်တည့်သွားပါ	Shay-*th*ọ*h* tẹh-dẹ*h* thwā*h*: bā*h*
Second turning to the right	လက်ယာဘက်မှာဒုတိယလမ်းကိုလိုက်	Let-yā*h*-bet-hmā*h* dootëëyă*h* lă*h*n:-go*h* lik
Cross the road	လမ်းကိုကူးသွား	Lă*h*n:-go*h* koo:-thwā*h*:
In what street is ...?	— ဘယ်လမ်းတွင်ရှိသလဲ	— beh lă*h*n:-dwin shëe *th*ă*h*-leh
Please tell me the nearest way to...	— သို့ရောက်အောင်အနီးဆုံးလမ်းကိုပြောပါ။	— *th*ọ*h* yowk-owng ă*h*-nee:-zôh*n*: lă*h*n:-go*h* pyaw-bā*h*

English.	Burmese.	Pronunciation.
Is this the way to...?	သည်လမ်းကိုလိုက်လျှင် — သို့ရောက်နိုင်ပါမည်လား	*Th*ee lă*h*n:-go*h* lik-hlyin — *thọh*-yowk-hning-bā*h*-mĕĕ-lā*h*:
Do you know Mr. F.?	F. သခင်ကိုသိကျွမ်းသလား	F. thă*h*hken-go*h* thēē-kyoon:-*thăh*-lā*h*:
I do not know	မသိသူး	Mă*h* thĕĕ-boo:
I know him well	သူကိုကောင်းကောင်းကျွမ်းသည်	Thŏŏ-go*h* kowng:-gowng: kyoon:-*th*ĕĕ
Who is he?	ထိုလူဘယ်လူလဲ	Hto*h* loo bă*h*loo leh
He is an old friend	သူမိတ်ဆွေဟောင်းဖြစ်ပါသည်	Thoo maytsway howng: hpyit-pā*h*-*th*ĕĕ
Where does he live?	သူဘယ်မှာနေသလဲ	Thoo beh-hmā*h* nay-*thăh*-leh
He lives close by (my home)	ကျွန်ုပ်အိမ်နှင့်အနီးနေပါသည်	(Kyŏŏno*h*k ayn-hnin) ă*h*-nee: nay-bā*h*-*th*ĕĕ
Is Mr. F. (Mrs. F.) at home?	F. သခင် (F. သခင်မ) အိမ်တွင်ရှိသလား	F. thă*h*hken (thă*h*-hken-mă*h*) ayn-dwin shēē-*thăh*-*lāh*:
I must go	ကျွန်ုပ်သွားပါတော့မည်	Kyŏŏno*h*k thwā*h*:-bā*h*-daw-mēē
Good-bye (go and return)	သွားဦးလော (*or* တော့)	Thwā*h*:-ō*h*n:-law (*or* daw)
What is the name of that street?	ထိုလမ်းကိုဘယ်နှယ်ခေါ်သလဲ	Hto*h* lă*h*n:-go*h* beh-hneh hkāw-*thăh*-leh

English.	Burmese.	Pronunciation.
Which road must I take?	ဘယ်လမ်းသွားရမည်လဲ	Beh lăhn: thwāh:-yăh-mëë-leh
(You) are out of the way	လမ်းမှားပြီ	Lăhn: hmāh: byee

Shopping. ဆိုင်များတွင်လှည့်ဝယ်ရာ။

English.	Burmese.	Pronunciation.
Howmuch is this?	သည်ဟာအဘိုးဘယ်လောက်လဲ	*Th*ee hā*h* ă*h*-hpô*h*: beh-lowk leh
It is too much	အဘိုးကြီးသည်	Ă*h*-hpô*h*: kee:-*th*ëë
Send them at once	ချက်ချင်းပို့လိုက်ပါ	Chet-chin: po*h̥*-lik-pā*h*
I wish to buy	ဝယ်ချင်သည်	Weh-jin-*th*ëë
(I) will take this	သည်ဟာကိုယူပါမည်	*Th*ee hā*h*-go*h* yoo-bā*h*-mëë
(I)wantsomecalico	ပိတ်ဝယ်ချင်သည်	Payt weh-jin-*th*ëë
Show (me) some ribbons	ပိုးကြိုးပြားတချို့ပြပါ	Pô*h*: kyô*h*:-byā*h* tă*h*-cho̥*h* pyă*h*-bā*h*
This colour is too dark	ဤအရောင်ညို့လွန်းသည်	Ee ă*h*-yowng nyo*h*-loon:-*th*ëë
Have you any that is narrower than this?	ဤကြိုးပြားထက်ပြက်ငယ်သောကြိုးပြားရှိသေးသလား	Ee kyô*h*:-byā*h*: det byet-gneh - *th*aw kyô*h*:-byā*h*: shëë-*th*ay:-*th*ă*h*-lā*h*:
What is the price per yard?	တကိုက်လျှင်အဘိုးဘယ်လောက်လဲ	Tă*h*-gik hlyin ă*h*-hpô*h*: beh-lowk leh
It is faded	အရောင်မှိန်သည်	Ă*h*-yowng hmayn-*th*ëë
It is too fine	အလွန်ညက်နုသည်	Ă*h*-hlöön nyet-nöö *th*ëë
This is right	သည်ဟာကောင်းသည်	*Th*ee hā*h* kowng:-*th*ëë

English.	Burmese.	Pronunciation.
What are they the pair?	တရံလျှင်အဘိုးဘယ် လောက်လဲ	Tá*h*-yă*h*n hlyin ă*h*-hpô*h*: beh-lowk leh
Have you any silk [1]putsoes for sale?	ပိုးပုဆိုးများရောင်း ရန်ရှိသလား	Pô*h*:-pă*h*sô*h*:-myā*h*: yowng:-yă*h*n shĕĕ-*th*ă*h*-lā*h*:
I will inquire and let you know	ကျွန်ုပ်မေးစစ်၍ကြား ပြောလိုက်မည်	Kyŏŏno*h*k may:-tsit-yŏğay kyā*h*:-pyaw-lik-mëë
I will give five rupees for it	ထိုဟာဘို့ငွေငါးကျပ် ပေးမည်	Hto*h* hā*h*-bo*h* gnway gnā*h*:-jă*h*t pay:-mëë
Take this watch to be mended	ဤနာရီခွက်ကိုပြင် ရအောင်ယူသွား လိုက်ပါ	Ee nā*h*yee-gwet-ko*h* pyin-yă*h*-owng yoo-thwā*h*:-lik-pā*h*
Can you give me change for a rupee?	ဒင်္ဂါးတကျပ်ကိုအန်း နှိုင်ပါမည်လား	Dingā*h*: tă*h*-jă*h*t-ko*h* ă*h*n: hning-bā*h*-mĕĕ-lā*h*:
I have no change	အန်းရန်မရှိပါ	Ă*h*n:-yă*h*n mă*h*-shëë bă*h*
I have no coppers, only four-anna pieces	ပိုက်ဆံမရှိပါ။ မတ် စေ့သာရှိပါသည်	Pisă*h*n mă*h* shĕĕ-bā*h*, mă*h*t tsĕğ *th*ā*h* shëë-bă*h*-*th*ĕĕ

Shooting and Fishing.

အမည်းငါး။ လိုက်၊ ပြစ်။ မျှားယူကြောင်း။

Is there any shooting or fishing here?	သည်အရပ်၌အမည်း ပြစ်ခင်း၊ ငါးမျှား ခင်းရှိသလား	*Th*ee ă*h*-yă*h*t hnik ă*h*-meh: pit hkin:, hgnā*h*: hmyā*h*:-gin shĕĕ-*th*ă*h*-lā*h*:

[1] The garment worn by men round the waist; some are very handsome.

English.	Burmese.	Pronunciation.
Can you find me a hunter?	မုဆိုးတယောက်ရှားပေးနိုင်ပါမည်လား	Mo*h*ksô*h*: tă*h*-yowk shā*h*: pay: hning-bă*h*-mëë-lā*h*:
I will send you a hunter to show you game?	အမည်းကိုညွှန်ပြရအောင်မုဆိုးတယောက်ကိုခေါ်ပေးမည်	Ă*h*-meh:-go*h* hnyŏŏn-pyă*h*-yă*h*-owng mo*h*ksô*h*: tă*h*-yowk-ko*h* hkāw-pay:-mëë
What game can you show me?	ဘယ်အမည်းမျိုးများကိုပြနိုင်ပါမည်လား	Beh ă*h*-meh:-myô*h*:-myā*h*:-go*h* pyă*h* hning-bā*h*-mëë-lā*h*:
Do you wish to shoot deer or birds?	ဆတ် သမင်၊ ဒရယ်၊ ဂျီများကိုပစ်ချင်သလား။ ငှက်များကိုပစ်ချင်သလား	Să*h*t, thă*h*min, dă*h*-yeh, jee-myā*h*:-go*h* pit-chin-*th*ă*h*-lă*h*:; hgnet-myā*h*:-go*h* pit-chin-*th*ă*h*-lă*h*:
There are plenty of hog deer in the jungle and sometimes one finds hares and pigs	တောထဲမှာဒရယ်အလွန်များသည်။ ငှင်းပြင်တခါတလေယုံနှင့်တောဝက်များတွေ့ထတ်သည်	Taw-deh-hmā*h* dă*h*-yeh ă*h*-hlŏŏn myā*h*:-*th*ëë; lă*h*-gowng:-pyin tă*h*-hkā*h*-tă*h*-lay yo*h*n-hnin̥ taw-wet-myā*h*: twa̩y-dă*h*t-thëë
Snipe are found in the rice fields and duck and teal in the lake	လယ်ပြင်ထဲမှာမြေဝတ်များပေါသည်။ အင်းထဲမှာဝမ်းဘဲနှင့်စစ်စလီကိုတွေ့ထိမ့်မည်	Leh-byin-deh-hmā*h* myay-wŏŏt-myā*h*:-paw-*th*ëë; in:-deh-hmā*h* woom:-beh-hnin̥ tsitsă*h*lee-go*h* twa̩y-la̩ym-mëë

English.	Burmese.	Pronunciation.
Is the jungle very thick?	တောများစွာရှုပ်တတ်သလား	Taw myāh: - zŏŏāh shohk-tăht-thăh-lāh:
The tree jungle is not thick but there is tall grass near the river	သစ်တောမရှုပ်ဘူး။ ထိုရာတွင်မြစ်ကမ်းနှင့်မြက်တောရှိသည်	Thit-taw măh-shohk-hpoo:; tho̥h-yāh-dwin, myit-kăhn: - hnik myet-taw shĕĕ-thĕĕ
How many guns have you?	သေနတ်ဘယ်နှစ်လက်ရှိသလဲ	Thay-năht beh-hnăh-let shĕĕ-thăh-leh
I have three double-barrel and a rifle	နှစ်လုံးပြူသေနတ်သုံးလက်နှင့်ရိုက်ပတ်တလက်ရှိသည်	Hnăh-lôhn:-byŏŏ-thay-năht thôhn:-let-hni̥n yikpăht tăh-let shĕĕ-thĕĕ
This gun is a breechloader	သည်သေနတ်နောက်ထိုးသေနတ်ဖြစ်ပါသည်	Thee thay-năht nowk-htôh: - thăy-năht hpyit-pāh-thĕĕ
How many cartridges have you in that bag?	ထိုလွယ်အိပ်ထဲမှာယမ်းတောင့်ဘယ်နှစ်လုံးပါသလဲ	Htoh lweh-ayk - deh-hmāh yăhn:- dowṇg beh-hnăh-lôhn: pāh-thăh-leh
Put sixty cartridges into that box	ထိုသစ်တာထဲမှာယမ်းတောင့်ခြောက်ဆယ်လောက်ထည့်လိုက်	Htoh thit-tăh-deh-hmāh yăhn:-dowṇg chowk - seh - lowk hteḥ-lik
You have hit (shot) a red deer, Sir	ဆတ်တကောင်ကိုမှန်ပါပြီသခင်	Săht tăh-gowng-goh hmăhn - bāh - byee, thăhhken
It cannot go far, for its leg is broken	ခြေထောက်ကျိုးလို့ဝေးစွာမသွားနိုင်ဘူး	Chay-dowk kyôh: lo̥h way - zŏŏāh măh thwāh:-hning-boo:

English.	Burmese.	Pronunciation
A teal has fallen in the grass near the pond	စစ်စလီတကောင် အိုင်နားမှာမြက်ပင်ထဲသို့ကျလေပြီ	Tsitsă*h*lee tă*h*-gowng ing-nā*h*:-hmā*h* myet-pin-deh-*th*o̥*h* kyă*h*-lay-byee
There are some jungle-fowl in the bamboos	ဝါးတောထဲမှာတောကြက်များရှိသည်	Wā*h*:-daw-deh-hmā*h* taw-jet-myā*h*: shĕĕ-*th*ĕĕ
Can you catch fish in that stream?	ထိုချောင်းတွင်ငါးများကိုမျှားနိုင်သလား	Hto*h* chowng:-dwin gnā*h*:-myā*h*:-go*h* hmyā*h*:-hning-*th*ă*h*-lā*h*:
What is the best bait?	မျှားစာအကောင်းဆုံးဘယ်သင်းလဲ	Hmyā*h*:-zā*h* ă*h*-kowng:-zô*h*n: beh-*th*in: leh
Bring a rod and some bait with you	မျှားတံတစင်းနှင့်မျှားစာအချို့ယူလာခဲ့	Hmyā*h*:-dă*h*n-tă*h*-zin:-hnin̥ hmyā*h*:-zā*h* ă*h*-cho̥*h* yoo-lā*h*-geh̥
The best bait is worms and maggots	တီနှင့်လောက်များ မျှားစာအကောင်းဆုံးဖြစ်သည်	Tee-hnin̥ lowk-myā*h*: hmyā*h*:-zā*h* ă*h*-kowng:-zô*h*n: hpyit-thëë
If you cannot get them, use paste	၎င်းကိုမရနိုင်လျှင် မုန့်စိမ်းကိုသုံး	Lă*h*-gowng:-go*h* mă*h* yă*h*-hning-hlyin, mo*h*n̥-zayn: go*h* thô*h*n:
You cannot hunt tigers without elephants	ဆင်မရှိလျှင်ကျားများကိုမလိုက်နိုင်ဘူး	Sin mă*h* shëë-hlyin, kyā*h*:-myā*h*:-go*h* mă*h* lik-hning-boo:

English.	Burmese.	Pronunciation.
You can watch for them at night on a stage in a tree	ညအခါသစ်ပင်ပေါ် ကလင့်စင်မှာစောင့် နေနိုင်သည်	Nyah ah-hkāh thit-pin-bāw-găh liṉ-zin hmāh tsowṉg-nay-hning-*th*ēē
It is, however, weary work and the mosquitoes bite	သို့ရာတွင်အလွန်ပင် ပန်း၍ခြင်ကိုက် သည့်	*Th*ọh-yāh-dwin, ăh-hlŏŏn pim-băhn:-yŏŏṉay chin kik-thee
How long have you lived in this circle ?[1]	သည်တိုက်ထဲမှာ နေသည့်ဟာဘယ် လောက်ကြာပြီလဲ	*Th*ee tik-hteh-hmāh nay-*th*ăh-hāh beh-lowk kyāh-byee-leh

Public Works. မြေတိုင်း၊တည်ဆောက်သောအရာများ။

Come here with your hoe	ပေါက်တူးကိုယူ၍ သည်ကိုလာကဲ့	Powk-too:-goh yoo-yŏṉay dee-goh lāh-geḥ
Do not dig there	ဟိုမှာမတူးနှင့်	Hoh-hmūh măh too:-hniṉ
Dig wider	ကျယ်အောင်တူး လိုက်	Kyeh-owng too:-lik
How many men are wanted to cut the jungle ?	တောခုတ်ရအောင် လူဘယ်နှစ်ယောက် အလိုရှိသလဲ	Taw hkohk-yăh-owng loo beh-hnăh yowk ăh-loh shēē-*th*ăh-leh

[1] NOTE.—တိုက် tik, generally translated *circle*, corresponds to our word 'hundred' in the divisions of a county. The word ဟာ hāh, *thing*, which occurs in the last sentence, is a very common colloquial idiom and corresponds to our word *fact*.

English.	Burmese.	Pronunciation.
Six men are wanted for road work	လမ်းလုပ်ရန်လူခြောက်ယောက်လိုချင်သည်	La*h*n: lo*h*k-ya*h*n loo-chowk-yowk lo*h*-jin-*th*ee
Send three men to help the carpenters	လက်သမားများကိုကူညီရအောင်လူသုံးယောက်ကိုလွှတ်လိုက်	Letthă*h*mā*h*:-myā*h*:-go*h* koo-nyee-yăh-owng loo-thô*h*n:-yowk-ko*h* hlŏŏt-lik
Take seven men to build the bridge	တံတားဆောက်ရန်လူခုနှစ်ယောက်ခေါ်သွားတော့	Tá*h*-dā*h*: sowk-yă*h*n loo hkŏŏhnă*h*-yowk hkaw-thwā*h*:-daw
What kind of soil is it there?	ထိုမှာဘယ်မြေမျိုးရှိသလဲ	Ho*h*-hmā*h* beh myay myô*h*: shĕĕ-*th*ă*h*-leh
It is sandy, Sir	သဲမြေများပါသည်သခင်	Theh-myay myā*h*:-bā*h*-*th*ĕĕ, thă*h*hken
Where did you find this stiff clay?	သည်မြေစေးကိုဘယ်မှာတွေ့သလဲ	*Th*ee myay-zay:-go*h* beh-hmā*h* tway-*th*ă*h*-leh
This ground is exceedingly hard	သည်မြေအလွန်ထရောမာပါသည်	*Th*ee myay ă*h*hlŏŏn-dă*h*-yā*h* mā*h*-bā*h*-*th*ëë
The hoe will break, so get a pickaxe	ပေါက်တူးကြိုးမည်စိုးလို့ပေါက်တူးလုံးတလက်ကိုယူကဲ့	Powk-too: kyô*h*:-mëe tso*h*:-lo*h* powk-too:-lô*h*n: tă*h*-let-ko*h* yoo-geh
Remove the stones with a crowbar	ကျောက်များကိုသံတူးရှင်းနှင့်တူးဆွလိုက်	Kyowk-myā*h*:-go*h* thă*h*n-tă*h*-yŏŏin:-hnin too:-swă*h*-lik

English.	Burmese.	Pronunciation.
Blast the rock	ကျောက်ကြီးကိုယမ်းနှင့်ဖေါက်ခွဲ	Kyowk - kee: - go*h* yă*h*n: - hniṉ hpowk-hkweh
Putaside all stones fit for building	အဆောက်အဦးနှင့်တော်သောကျောက်များကိုတဘက်မှာစုပုံလိုက်	Ă*h*-sowk ä*h*-ô*h*n:-hniṉ tāw-*th*aw kyowk-myā*h*:-go*h* tă*h*-hpet-hmā*h* tsŏŏ-po*h*n-lik
The space is not sufficient	ထားရန်နေရာမလောက်ဘူး	Htā*h*:-yă*h*n nay-yā*h* mă*h* lowk hpoo:
Level 30 ft. further back	ပေ၃၀လောက်နောက်သို့တိုး၍ညီညာအောင်ပြုလုပ်ပါ	Pay thô*h*n:-zeh lowk nowk-*thoh* tô*h*:-yŏŏay nyee-nyā*h*-owng pyŏŏ-lo*h*k-pā*h*
When I called you, why did you not answer?	သင့်ကိုခေါ်ကာသာဘာပြုလို့မထူးသလဲ	*Th*iṉ-go*h* hkāw kā*h*lă*h* bā*h*-pyŏŏ-loḫ mă*h* htoo:-*th*ă*h*-leh
As the ground is very soft you must lay planks	မြေအလွန်ပျော့သည်နှင့်ပျဉ်ပြားများကိုခင်းချရမည်	Myay ă*h*-hlŏŏn pyaw-*th*ĕë-hniṉ pyeen-byă*h*:-myā*h*:-go*h* hkin:-chă*h*-yă*h*-mĕë
Bring the cord and pegs for laying out the foundation	အခြေအလျာကိုမှတ်ချရန်ကြိုးနှင့်ပန်နက်များယူခဲ့	Ă*h*-chay ă*h*-lyā*h*-go*h* hmă*h*t-chă*h*-yă*h*n kyô*h*:-hniṉ pă*h*net myu*h*: yoo-geḫ
Must this work be finished to-day?	သည်အလုပ်ယနေ့ပြီးအောင်လုပ်ရမည်လား	*Th*ee ă*h*-lo*h*k yă*h*-nay pyee: - owng lo*h*k - yă*h*-mĕë-lā*h*:
There is not enough sand in this mortar	သည်သရွတ်တွင်သဲမလောက်ဘူး	*Th*ee thă*h*yŏŏt-twin theh mă*h* lowk hpoo:

English.	Burmese.	Pronunciation.
There is too much lime in it	သရွတ်တွင်ထုံးများလွန်းသည်	Thă*h*yŏŏt-twin htô*h*n: myā*h*:-loon:-*th*ëë
The lime is not good. What kiln did it come from?	ထုံးမကောင်းဘူး။ ထုံးဖိုမှတယ်လဲ	Htô*h*n: mă*h* kowng: boo: ; beh htô*h*n:-bo*h*-hmă*h* leh
The plastering must be done carefully	အင်္ဂတေကိုင်သည်မှာ သေသေချာချာပြုရမည်	Ingă*h*day king-*th*ëë hmā*h*, thay-*th*ay chā*h*-jā*h* pyŏŏ-yă*h*-mëë
Unless the timber is properly earth-oiled the white ants will eat it	သစ်သားကိုရေနံ ကောင်းကောင်းမ သုတ်လျှင်ခြများ တက်စားလိမ့်မည်	Thit-thā*h*:-go*h* yay-nă*h*n kowng:-gowng: mă*h* tho*h*k-hlyin chă*h*-myāh: tet-tsā*h*:-laymmëë
White ants do not eat iron-wood or teak	ကျွန်းသစ်နှင့်ပျဉ်းကတိုး ခြများမစား တတ်ဘူး	Kyŏŏn-*th*it-hnin pyin:-gă*h*-dô*h*: chă*h*-myā*h*: mă*h* tsā*h*:-dă*h*t-hpoo:
Will you have thatch or shingles on the roof?	ဒနီဖက်နှင့်သက် ကယ်မိုးမည်လား။ သို့မဟုတ်ပျဉ် အုပ်ကြွတ်နှင့်မိုး မည်လား	Dă*h*nëë-bet-hnin thek-keh mô*h*:-mëë-lā*h*: ; *th*o*h*-mă*h*-ho*h*k, py-een o*h*k-kyŏŏt-hnin mô*h*:-mëë-lā*h*:
Tiles are difficult to obtain	အုတ်ကြွတ်များထယ် ရခဲသည်	O*h*k-kyŏŏt-myā*h*: teh yă*h*-geh-*th*ëë
Bring me the compass and chain	ကွန်ပါနှင့်မြေတိုင်း သံကြိုးကိုယူလာခဲ့	Kŏŏmpā*h*-hnin myay-ding-thă*h*n-jô*h*:-go*h* yoo-lā*h*-geh

English.	Burmese.	Pronunciation.
I forgot them and left them in the works office	မေ့လျော့လို့မြေတိုင်းရုံးမှာကျန်ရစ်နေသည်	Mạy-yạw-lọ*h* myay-ding-yo*h*n-hmā*h* kyă*h*n-yit nay-*th*ëë

Planting. သစ်ပင်စိုက်ခြင်း။

English.	Burmese.	Pronunciation.
How many coolies have you?	ကူလီဘယ်နှစ်ယောက်ရှိသလဲ	Koolee beh-hnă*h*-yowk shëë-*thăh*-leh
How long have they worked with you?	သူတို့မောင်မင်းဆီမှာလုပ်သဟာဘယ်လောက်ကြာပြီလဲ	Thoo-dọ*h* mowng-min:-zee-hmā*h* lo*h*k thă*h*-hā*h* beh-lowk kyū*h*-byee-leh
Are they good workers?	အလုပ်ကိုဝီရိယနှင့်လုပ်တတ်ကြသလား	Ă*h*-lo*h*k-ko*h* wĕĕyĕĕ-yă*h*-hnịn lo*h*k-tă*h*t-kyă*h*-*thăh*-lāh:
Muster the coolies near the bungalow	အိမ်နားမှာကူလီများကိုစုရုံး၍ထားလိုက်	Ayn-nā*h*:-hmā*h* koo-lee-myā*h*:-go*h* tsŏŏ-yô*h*n:-yŏọay htā*h*:-lik
How much pay does each get a day?	ကူလီများတကိုယ်လျှင်နေ့တိုင်းအခဘယ်လောက်ရတတ်သလဲ	Koolee-myā*h*: tă*h*-gô*h*-hlyin nạy-ding: ă*h*-hkă*h* beh-lowk yă*h*-dă*h*t-thă*h*-leh
Each man must dig forty holes a day?	ကူလီတယောက်တနေ့လျှင်တွင်းလေးဆယ်စီတူးရမည်	Koolee-tă*h*-yowk ta*h*-nạy-hlyin twin: lay:-zeh zee too:-yă*h*-mĕĕ
Do not pull up the young plants	အပင်ကလေးများကိုဆွဲ၍မနှုတ်နှင့်	Ă*h*-pin-gă*h*lay:-myā*h*:-go*h* sweh-yŏọay mă*h*-hno*h*k-hnịn

English.	Burmese.	Pronunciation.
Mark the places where they are to dig the holes	တွင်းတူးရမည့်နေရာများကိုမှတ်ပြလိုက်	Twin: too:-yăh-mĕe-nay-yāh-myāh:-goh hmăht-pyăh-lik
Trample the earth down in planting	အပင်များကိုစိုက်ကာလ မြေကိုခြေနှင့်နှိတ်နင်းလိုက်	Ăh-pin-myāh:-goh tsik-kăhlăh, myay-goh chee-hnin hnayk-nin:-lik
Go and fetch the plants from the seed-beds	ပျိုးခင်းကအပင်ကလေးများကိုသွားယူခဲ့	Pyôh:-gin:-găh ăh-pin-găhlay:-myāh:-goh thwāh: yoo-geh
Take up the plants with the earth	အပင်ကိုမြေပါအောင်နှုတ်ပါ	Ăh-pin-goh myay pāh-owng hnohk-pāh
After planting them give them plenty of water	စိုက်ပြီးမှရေကောင်းကောင်းလောင်း၍ပေးလိုက်	Tsik-pyee:-hmăh yay kowng:-gowng: lowng:-yŏŏay pay:-lik

Arrival in the Country. ပြည်တွင်ရောက်ကာလ။

(For Vocabularies, see p. 61.)

Here is my luggage	ကျွန်နုပ်ဝန်စလယ်သည်ဤမှာရှိသည်	Kyŏŏnohk wŏŏn-zăh-leh dee-hmāh shĕĕ-thëë
Where is the custom-house?	အကောက်တိုက်ဘယ်မှာလဲ	Ăh-kowk-tik beh-hmāh leh
Bring that trunk to the custom-house	ယိုသေတ္တာအကောက်တိုက်သို့ယူခဲ့	Hoh thittāh ăh-kowk-tik-thoh yoo-geh
I have nothing dutiable	အကောက်ခွဲရန်ဥစ္စာမပါ	Ăh-kowk-hkweh-yăhn-ohksāh măh pāh

English.	Burmese.	Pronunciation.
Here are (take) my keys	ကျွန်ုပ်သော့များယူပါတော့	Kyŏŏn o*h*k thaw-myā*h*: yoo-bā*h*-daw
Call a carriage	ရထားတစီးခေါ်ပါ	Yă*h*htā*h*: tă*h*-zee: hkāw-bā*h*
There is no carriage	ရထားတစီးမျှမရှိပါ	Yă*h*htā*h*: tă*h*-zee:-hmyă*h* mă*h* shëé-bā*h*
What is the fare to —?	— သို့ အခ ဘယ်လောက်လဲ	— *th*ŏ*h* ă*h*-hkă*h* beh-lowk, leh
Tell the driver to take me to —	ရထားမှူးကို — သို့ မောင်းသွားလို့ ပြောလိုက်ပါ	Yă*h*htā*h*:-hmoo:-go*h* — *th*o*h* mowng:-thwā*h*:-lo*h* pyaw-lik-pā*h*
Tell him to drive quickly to the railway station	မီးရထားရုံသို့ မြန်မြန်မောင်းလို့ ပြောလိုက်ပါ	Mee:-yă*h*htā*h*:-yo*h*n-*th*ŏ*h* myă*h*n-myă*h*n mowng:-lo*h* pyaw-lik-pā*h*
He says the baggage is too heavy (for a carriage), it must be put on a cart	ဝန်စလယ်လေးလွန်းသည်နှင့် လှည်းပေါ်မှာတင်ရမည်တည်း	Wŏŏn-ză*h*-leh lay:-loon:-*th*ëë-hniŋ hleh:-bāw-hmā*h*-tin yă*h*-mëë, deh
You must take it to the station for Prome, not that for Pegu	ပြည်မြို့သို့သွားရန်မီး ရထားရုံကိုယူသွား ရမည်။ ပဲခူးမြို့သို့ ထွက်ရန်ရုံသို့မယူရ	Pyee-myo*h*-*th*o*h* thwā*h*:-yă*h*n mee:-yă*h*htā*h*:-yo*h*n-go*h* yoo-thwā*h*:-yă*h*-mëë; Pă*h*gô*h*:-myo*h*-*th*o*h* htwet-yă*h*n yo*h*n-*th*o*h* mă*h* yoo-yă*h*

English.	Burmese.	Pronunciation.
I wish to catch the steamer that goes from Prome to Bamaw	ပြည်မြို့ကဘမော်မြို့သို့သွားသောမီးသင်္ဘောကိုမှီအောင်သွားချင်သည်	Pyee-myo̤*h*-gă*h* Bă*h*-maw-myo̤*h*-*th*o̤*h* thwă*h*:-*th*aw-mee:-thim:-baw-go*h*hmee-owng thwă*h*:-jin-*th*ëë
When does the steamer start?	မီးသင်္ဘောဘယ်အချိန်လောက်ထွက်သလဲ	Mee:-thim:baw beh-ă*h*-chayn-lowk htwet-thă*h*-leh
Please show me my berth	ကျွန်ုပ်အခန်းကိုပြလိုက်ပါ	Kyŏŏno*h*k ă*h*-hkă*h*n:-go*h* pyă*h*-lik-pă*h*
Is this berth taken?	သည်အခန်းကိုတစုံတယောက်ကယူပြီလား	Thee ă*h*-hkă*h*n:-go*h* tă*h*-zo*h*n-tă*h*-yowk-kă*h* yoo-byee-lă*h*:
I will engage the whole cabin	ကျွန်ုပ်တခန်းလုံးကိုယူပါမည်	Kyŏŏno*h*k tă*h*-hkă*h*n:-lô*h*n:-go*h* yoo-bă*h*-mëë
Put this bag in the cabin	သည်အိတ်ကိုအခန်းထဲမှာထားလိုက်	*Th*ee ayk-ko*h* ă*h*-hkă*h*n:-deh-hmă*h* htă*h*:-lik
What is the number of your cabin?	အခန်းနံပါတ်ဘာလဲ [လဲ	Ă*h*-hkă*h*n: nă*h*mbă*h*t bă*h* leh [leh
What is the fare?	ကတို့ခဘယ်လောက်	Kă*h*-do̤*h*-gă*h* beh-lowk,
How many days is it from Prome to Bamaw?	ပြည်မြို့ကဘမော်မြို့ရောက်အောင်ဘယ်နှစ်ရက်လောက်ရှိမည်လဲ	Pyee-myo̤*h*-gă*h* Bă*h*-maw-myo̤*h* yowk-owng beh-hnă*h* yet lowk shëë-mëë-leh
Are the mosquitoes troublesome (do they bite)?	ခြင်ကိုက်တတ်သလား	Chin kik-tă*h*t thă*h*-lă*h*:

English.	Burmese.	Pronunciation.
They do not bite in the cold season—only in the rains	ဆောင်းဥတု၌မကိုက်ဖူး။ မိုးဥတု၌သာကိုက်တတ်သည်	Sowng: ŏŏdŏŏ-hnik măh kik-hpoo:; môh: ŏŏdŏŏ-hnik *thāh* kik-tă*h*t-thēē
Have they mosquito curtains on board, or should I buy them?	သင်္ဘောမှာခြင်ထောင်ရှိသလား။ သို့မဟုတ်ဝယ်ရန်ကောင်းမည်လား	Thim:baw-hmā*h* chin-downg shēē-*thăh*-lā*h*:; *thoh*-mă*h*-ho*h*k, weh-yă*h*n kowng:-mĕĕ-lā*h*:
They had better be bought in Rangoon as they will be useful after leaving the boat	မီးသင်္ဘောကဆင်းပြီးမှများစွာအသုံးကျသည့်နှင့်ရန်ကုန်မြို့တွင်ဝယ်ရန်ကောင်းမည်	Mee:-thim:baw-gă*h* sin:-byee:-hmă*h* myā*h*:-zŏŏā*h* ă*h*thô*h*n:-kyă*h*-*th*ēĕ-hnin Yă*h*ngo*h*n-myo*h*-dwin weh-yă*h*n kowng:-mĕĕ
What do you call that pagoda on the other side of the river?	မြစ်ဟိုဖက်မှာရှိသည့်ဘုရားကိုဘယ်နှယ်ခေါ်သလဲ	Myit ho*h*-bet-hmā*h* shēē-*th*ēĕ hpă*h*-yā*h*:-go*h* beh-hneh hkāw-*thăh*-leh
Where is the Shway Dă*h*go*h*n Pagoda?	ရွှေဒဂုံဘုရားဘယ်မှာလဲ	Shway-Dă*h*go*h*n hpă*h*-yā*h*: beh-hmā*h*, leh
Can you buy me a good pony?	ကျွန်ုပ်ဖို့မြင်းကောင်းတကောင်ကိုဝယ်နိုင်ပါမည်လား	Kyŏŏno*h*k-hpo*h* myin:-gowng: tă*h*-gowng-go*h* weh-hning-bā*h*-mēē-lā*h*:
Do they shoe the ponies?	မြင်းများကိုသံခွာတတ်သလား	Myin:-myā*h*:-go*h* thă*h*n-hkwā*h* tă*h*t thă*h*-lā*h*:

English.	Burmese.	Pronunciation.
Saddle the pony	မြင်းကိုကုန်းနှီးတင်ခဲ့ပါ	Myin:-go*h* kô*h*n:-hnee: tin-geḫ-bā*h*
(I) wish to engage a Burmese servant	မြန်မာလူကလေးတယောက်ကိုငှါးချင်သည်	Bă*h*mā*h* loo-gă*h*-lay: tă*h*-yowk-ko*h* hgnā*h*:-jin-*th*ĕĕ
What wages does he ask?	လခဘယ်လောက်တောင်းသလဲ	Lă*h*-gă*h* beh-lowk towng:-*th*ă*h*-leh

Note—On arrival in the country a servant is required. It is usual to engage a native of India who speaks English.

The Railway. မီးရထားလမ်း

(For Vocabulary, see p. 61.)

English.	Burmese.	Pronunciation.
To the station	မီးရထားရုံကို	Mee:-yă*h*htā*h*:-yo*h*n-go*h*
Here is my luggage	ကျွန်ုပ်ဝန်စလည်သည်မှာရှိသည်	Kyŏŏno*h*k wŏŏnză*h*leh dee-hmā*h* shĕĕ-*th*ĕĕ
I wish to register my luggage for —	ကျွန်ုပ်ဝန်စလည်ကို ရီဂျစ္စရီလုပ်ချင်သည်	Kyŏŏno*h*k wŏŏnză*h*-leh-go*h* [1]ree-jiṭ-tsă*h*-ree lo*h*k-chin-*th*ĕĕ
The luggage is over weight	ဝန်အချိန်ပိုသည်	Wŏŏn ă*h*-chayn po*h*-*th*ĕĕ
Get my luggage	ကျွန်ုပ်ဝန်ကိုယူပေးပါ	Kyŏŏno*h*k wŏŏn-go*h* yoo-pay:-bā*h*
Here is the ticket	လက်မှတ်သည်မှာရှိသည်	Let-hmă*h*t dee-hmā*h* shĕĕ-*th*ĕĕ

[1] In foreign words it is often necessary to use ရ rā*h* as r and not y.

English.	Burmese.	Pronunciation.
How many packages are there?	အထုပ်ဘယ်နှထုပ်လဲ	Ă*h*-hto*h*k beh-hnă*h*-[1]hto*h*k, leh
Where is the waiting-room?	စောင့်ခန်းဘယ်မှာလဲ	Tsoyng-gă*h*n: beh-hmā*h*, leh
Where is the booking office?	လက်မှတ်ခံရုံဘယ်မှာလဲ	Let-hmă*ht*-hkă*h*n-yo*h*n beh-hmā*h*[2] leh
Where is the refreshment room?	စားပွဲခန်းဘယ်မှာလဲ	Tsă*h*-bweh-gă*h*n: beh-hmā*h*, leh
Where is the lavatory?	နောက်ဖေးဘယ်မှာလဲ	Nowk-hpay:[3] beh-hmā*h*, leh
Where is the train for —?	— ကိုသွားသောရထားဘယ်မှာရှိသလဲ	— go*h* thwā*h*:-*th*aw-yă*h*htā*h*: beh-hmā*h* shēē-*th*ă*h*-leh
Are you going by the express?	အမြန်ရထားနှင့်သွားမည်လား	Ă*h*-myă*h*n-yă*h*htā*h*:-hniņ thwā*h*:-mēē-lā*h*:
Show me a time-table	အချိန်ဇယားကွက်ကိုပြပါ	Ă*h*-chayn-ză*h*-yā*h*:-gwet-ko*h* pyă*h*-bā*h*
When does the train start?	ရထားဘယ်တော့ထွက်သလဲ	Yă*h*htā*h*: [4] behday htwet-thă*h*-leh
Can I book through to —?	— ကိုထောက်ရှောက်လက်မှတ်ခံနိုင်သလား	— go*h* dowk-showk-let-hmă*h*t hkă*h*n-ning-*th*ă*h*-lā*h*:

[1] Here is an example of the noun spoken of being used as its own numeral auxiliary instead of one of those given on pp. 79, 80.

[2] The verb ရှိ shēē is often omitted.

[3] နောက်ဖေး nowk-hpay: really means the back precincts of a house, i. e. rear.

[4] ဘယ်တော့ beh-day is a contracted form of ဘယ်သောအခါ beh *th*aw-ă*h*-hkā*h*.

English.	Burmese.	Pronunciation.
A first- (second-) class single ticket to —	— ကိုပဌမ (ဒုတိယ) တမ်းအသွားလက်မှတ်တစောင်လား	go*h* pä*h*-htä*h*mä*h* (dŏŏtëëyä*h*) dä*h*n: ä*h*-thwā*h*:-let-hmä*h*t tä*h*-zowng, lā*h*:
Return ticket	အသွားအပြန်လက်မှတ်	Ă*h*-thwā*h*:-ä*h*-pyä*h*n-let-hmä*h*t
How much is it?	ဘယ်လောက်လဲ	Beh-lowk, leh
We want a sleeping carriage	အိပ်ရန်ရထားကျွန်ုပ်တို့လိုသည်	Ayk-yä*h*n-yä*h*htā*h*: kyŏŏno*h*k-do*h* lo*h*-*th*ëë
A non-smoking compartment	ဆေးလိပ်မသောက်ရသောရထား	Say:-layk mä*h* thowk-yä*h*-*th*aw-yä*h*htā*h*:
Is this the train for —?	သည်ရထား—ကိုသွားရန်ရထားလား	*Th*ee yä*h*htā*h*: — go*h* thwā*h*:-yä*h*n yä*h*-htā*h*:, lā*h*:
Do I change anywhere?	တနေရာရာမှာရထားပြောင်းရမည်လား	Tä*h*-nay-yā*h*-yā*h*-hmā*h* yä*h*htā*h*: pyowng-yä*h*-mëë-lā*h*:
Where must I change for —?	— ကိုသွားရန်ဘယ်မှာရထားပြောင်းရမည်လဲ	— go*h* thwā*h*:-yä*h*n beh-hmā*h* yä*h*htā*h*: pyowng:-yä*h*-mëë-leh
Is this seat engaged?	သည်ထိုင်ရာလူယူပြီလား	*Th*ee hting-yā*h* loo yoo-byee-lā*h*: [boo:
There is no room	နေရာမရှိဘူး	Nay-yā*h* mä*h* shëë-
Call the guard	ဂတ်ဘိုကိုခေါ်ပါ	Gä*h*t-bo*h*-go*h* hkāw-bā*h*
The train is just going to start	ရထားယခုဘဲထွက်မည်	Yä*h*htā*h*: yä*h*-hkŏŏ-beh htwet-mëë

English.	Burmese.	Pronunciation.
Open the door	တံခါးဖွင့်ပါ	Tá*h*-gā*h*: hpwiṇ-bā*h*
Open the window	ပြတင်းဖွင့်ပါ	Pă*h*-din: hpwiṇ-bā*h*
Here is the station	မီးရထားရုံသည်မှာရှိ သည်	Mee-yă*h*htā*h*:-yo*h*n dee-hmā*h* shĕĕ-*th*ĕĕ
Do we stop here?	သည်မှာရပ်သလား	Dee-hmā*h* yă*h*t-thă*h*-lā*h*:
Do we alight here?	သည်မှာဆင်းရမည် လား	Dee-hmā*h* sin:-yă*h*-mĕĕ-lā*h*:
Do we change carriages here?	သည်မှာရထားပြောင်း ရမည်လား	Dee-hmā*h* yă*h*htā*h*: pyowng:-yă*h*-mĕĕ-lā*h*:
How long do we stop here?	သည်မှာဘယ်လောက် ကြာရပ်သလဲ	Dee-hmā*h* beh-lowk-kyā*h* yă*h*t-thă*h*-leh
Five minutes	ငါးမိနစ်	Gnă*h*: mĕĕnit
My luggage is lost	ကျွန်ုပ်ဝန်ပျောက် သွားသည်	Kyŏŏnoh*k* wŏŏn pyowk-thwā*h*:-*th*ĕĕ
When it arrives forward it on to —	ရောက်သောအခါ — ကိုပို့ပါ	Yowk-thaw-ă*h*-hkā*h* — go*h* poh̥-bā*h*
Give me your ticket [To superior]	ခင်ဗျားလက်မှတ် ပေးပါ	Hkenbyā*h*: let-hmă*h*t pay:-bā*h*
[Do. to inferior]	မင်းလက်မှတ်ပေး	Min: let-hmă*h*t pay:
Here it is [To superior]	သည်မှာပါ	Dee-hmā*h* bā*h*
[Do. to inferior]	သည်မှာ	Dee-hmā*h*

Specimen of Burmese Handwriting.

*The Lord's Prayer.**

[Burmese is written from left to right, and the written characters are a copy of the printed ones, more or less close according to the skill and care of the writer. See p. 22.]

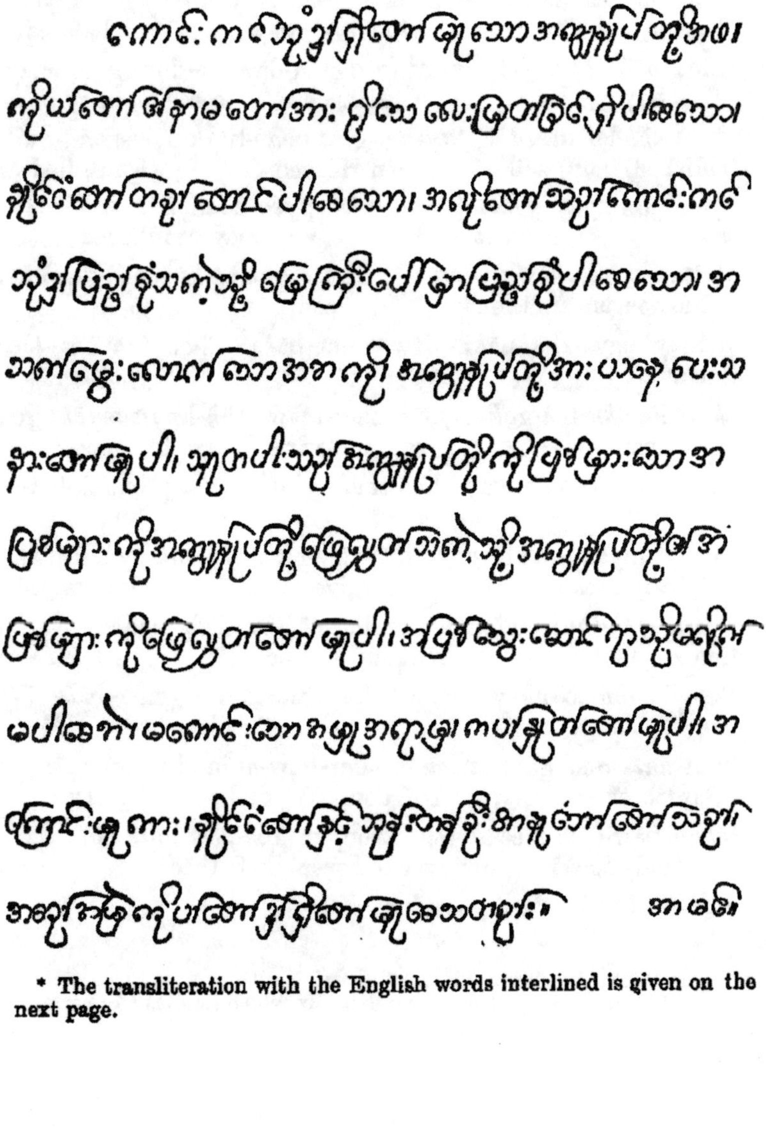

* The transliteration with the English words interlined is given on the next page.

The Lord's Prayer.

Transliteration of the Burmese words with the English translation.

Kowng:-gin-bo*h*n-hnik shëë-dāw-moo-*th*aw ă*h*-kyŏŏno*h*k-tọ*h*
In Heaven which art our

ă*h*-hpă*h*ı ko*h*dāw-ëë nā*h*mă*h*-dāw-ā*h*: yo*h*-*th*ay-lay:-myă*h*t-
Father, Thy name to hallowing

chin: shëë-bā*h*-zay-*th*aw॥ ning-ngă*h*n-dāw tee-downg-bā*h*-zay-
be; Kingdom come (*lit.* may be es-

*th*aw॥ ă*h*-lo*h*-dāw-*th*ëë kowng:-gin:-bo*h*n-hnik pyëë-zo*h*n-thă*h*-
tablished) (and) will in Heaven is fulfilled

gẹh-*th*ọ*h* myay-gyee:-bāw-hmā*h* pyëë-zo*h*n-bā*h*-zay-*th*aw॥
as on earth may be fulfilled;

ă*h*-thet-mway:-lowk-*th*aw ă*h*-sā*h*-go*h* ă*h*-kyŏŏno*h*k-tọ*h*-ā*h*:
life nourish sufficient food to us

yă*h*nạy pay:-thă*h*nā*h*:-dāw-moo-bā*h*॥ Thoo-tă*h*bā*h*:-*th*ëë
this day give; (by) others

ă*h*-kyŏŏno*h*k-tọ*h*-go*h* pyit-hmā*h*:-*th*aw ă*h*-hpyit-myā*h*:-go*h*
against us committed trespasses

ă*h*-kyŏŏno*h*k-tọ*h* hpyay-hlŏŏt-thă*h*-gẹh-*th*ọ*h* ă*h*-kyŏŏno*h*k-tọ*h*-ëë
we forgive as our

ă*h*-pyit-myā*h*:-go*h* hpyay-hlŏŏt-tāw-moo-bā*h*॥ ă*h*-pyit-thway:-
trespasses forgive: into tempta-

zowng-yā*h*-*th*ọ*h* mă*h* lik mă*h* pā*h*-zay-beh mă*h*-kowng:-
tion without leading from evil

*th*aw-ă*h*-*h*mŏŏ-ă*h*-yā*h*-hmă*h* keh-hno*h*k-tāw-moo-bā*h*॥ ă*h*-
things deliver (us).

kyowng:-moo-gā*h*: ning-nga*h*n-dāw-hnin hpo*h*n:-tă*h*go*h*:
For (these reasons); kingdom and glory

[1]ă*h*nŏŏbăw-dāw-*th*ëë ă*h*-tsin-ă*h*-myeh ko*h*-dāw-hnik shëë-dāw-
(and) power for ever and ever to thee. are.

moo-ëë-thă*h*dee:[2]॥ ā*h*min॥
Amen.

[1] Ā*h*nŏŏbăw is a Burmanised Pāli word.
[2] Thă*h*dee: is a very strong assertive affix which implies 'for certain'.

Money, Weights and Measures.

ကြေးငွေဒင်္ဂါး။ အလေးအချိန်နှင့်အတိုင်းအထွာများ။

Money. ဒင်္ဂါး။

The present coinage of Burma is the same as that used throughout British India.

BURMESE MONEY WITH THE ENGLISH AND AMERICAN VALUES.

(Subject to the fluctuations in the rate of exchange.)

NOTES.—English Bank-notes and Drafts are current.

GOLD COINS.—The English sovereign and half-sovereign are current and are not subject to the fluctuations in the rate of exchange.

SILVER COINS.

Burmese.		English.		American.
1 rupee	=	1s. 4*d.*	=	33 cents.
½ ”	=	8*d.*	=	16 ”
¼ ”	=	4*d.*	=	8 ”
⅛ ”	=	2*d.*	=	4 ”

NICKEL COIN.

1 anna	=	1*d.*	=	2 cents.

BRONZE COINS.

Burmese.		English.		American.
½ anna	=	½*d.*	=	1 cent.

Also ¼ anna, and 1/12 anna.

16 annas = 1 rupee.

15 rupees = £1.

ENGLISH AND AMERICAN MONEY REDUCED TO BURMESE.

£	s.	d.		Dols.	Cents.		Rupees.	Annas.
50	0	0	=	250	0	=	750	0
25	0	0	=	125	0	=	375	0
10	0	0	=	50	0	=	150	0
5	0	0	=	25	0	=	75	0
4	0	0	=	20	0	=	60	0
3	0	0	=	15	0	=	45	0
1	0	0	=	5	0	=	15	0
	10	0	=	2	50	=	7	8
	5	0	=	1	25	=	3	12
	4	0	=	1	0	=	3	0
	2	6	=		62½	=	1	14
	2	0	=		50	=	1	8
	1	0	=		25	=		12
		6	=		12½	=		6
		3	=		6	=		3
		1	=		2	=		1
		0½	=		1	=		0½
		0¼	=		0½	=		0¼

½ anna = 6 pies, ¼ anna = 3 pies.

Certain words applicable to the old system still come into use.

The Rupee is called ကျပ် kyăht.

½ Rupee	„	ငါးမူး gnāh:-moo:.
¼ „	„	မတ် măht.
⅛ „	„	မူး moo:.
$\frac{1}{16}$ „ (anna)	„	ပဲ peh.
$\frac{1}{12}$ Anna (pie)	„	ပိန် ping.

Note.—The mark ° over a numeral also denotes သိပ် thit and ပိုင် pi.

Rs. 506 ၊ 7 ။ 2 = ၅၀၆°–၇–၂, 506 rupees, 7 annas, and 2 pies.

All copper coins, however, are designated as ပိုက်ဆံ pi-săhn.

Correctly speaking the ½ rupee (eight-anna piece) should be လေးမူး lay:-moo:, but the old Burmese ကျပ် kyăht was worth more than the Indian rupee.

The numeral affix for all coins (except the rupee) is ပြား pyāh:, and for the rupee ကျပ် kyăht.

ပိုက်ဆံလေးပြား pi-săhn lay:-byāh:, four pies.

ဒင်္ဂါးလေးကျပ် dingāh: lay:-jăht, four rupees.

Eight annas may be either ရှစ်ပဲ shit-peh, or ငါးမူး gnāh:-moo:.

Four annas လေးပဲ lay:-beh, or တမတ် tăh-măht.

Before the country was annexed there was no coinage and silver was used by weight; the Burmese 'kyăht' is said to have been 252·75 grs. Troy.

Weights. အလေး။

The weights start with the ချင်ရွေး chin-yŏŏay:, still used by silversmiths. It is a small red seed of which there are two kinds, ချင်ရွေး chin-yooay:, *Abrus precatorius*, ရွေးကြီး yooay:-jee:, *Adinanthera pavonina*.

2 ချင်ရွေး chin-yŏŏay:	=	1	ရွေးကြီး yŏŏay-jee:.
3 ရွေးကြီး yŏŏay-jee:	=	1	ပဲ peh (pea).
2 ပဲ peh	=	1	မူး moo:.
2 မူး moo:	=	1	မတ် măht.
4 မတ် măht	=	1	ကျပ် kyăht.
5 ကျပ် kyăht	=	1	ဗိုလ် boh.
20 ဗိုလ် boh	=	1	ပိဿာ paykthāh, *or* အခွက် ăh-hkwet.

The paykthāh *viss* or *hkwet* is $3\frac{65}{100}$ lb. avoirdupois, or about 3 lb. 2 oz.

The term ခွက် hkwet is substituted for ပိဿာ paykthāh in connection with any capital number above ten; as, အခွက်နှစ်ဆယ် āh-hkwet-hnāh-seh, 20 viss.

In abbreviated writing

One peh is ဝဲ.	One māht is ပံ.
One moo: is ဍ.	One kyāht is ပိ.

Measures of Length.

The best to start from is the အသစ် āh-thit or finger's-breadth.

ငါးသစ် gnāh:-thit (5 thit)	= တမုတ် tāh-mohk (fist with thumb shut down).
ရှစ်သစ် shit-thit (8 thit)	= တမိုက် tāh-mik (fist with thumb stuck out).
ဆယ်နှစ်သစ် seh-hnāh-thit (12 thit)	= တထွာ tāh-htwāh (span).
နှစ်ထွာ hnāh-htwāh (2 htwāh)	= တတောင် tāh-downg (cubit)
လေးတောင် lay:-downg (4 cubits)	= တလံ tāh-lāhn (fathom).
ခုနှစ်တောင် hköö-hnāh-downg (7 cubits, sometimes 8 cubits)	= တတာ tāh-tāh.
တာထောင် tāh tāh-htowng (1000)	= တတိုင် tāh-ding.

The တိုင် ting is very nearly two English miles.

Now the English measures are generally used and understood.

Measures of Capacity.

၁ စလယ် 1 tsāh-leh =	(1 pint).
၄ စလယ် 4 tsāh-leh	= ၁ ပြည် 1 pyēē (half-gallon).
၂ ပြည် 2 pyēē	= ၁ စရွတ် 1 tsāh-yööt (1 gallon).
၂ စရွတ် 2 tsāh-yööt	= ၁ စိတ် 1 tsayt (2 gallons).
၂ စိတ် 2 tsayt	= ၁ ခွဲ 1 hkweh (half-bushel).
၂ ခွဲ 2 hkweh	= ၁ တင်း 1 tin: (2 bushel baskets).

Square Measure.

The English acre (ဧက aykăh) is now the standard, but the Burmese had what they called a ငါးတင်းကြဲ gnăh:-din:-jeh, or 'five basket sow', which was also called ပယ် peh and equalled 1200 square cubits or 1·75 acres

Measures of Time.

English measures of time are prevalent, but the old unit was the နာရီ năh-yee, which was probably the Pali နာဍီ nāhdee, or, နာဠီ nāhllee, a measure of capacity used like an hour-glass or water-clock. These vessels varied in shape, but the Burmese counted 60 to the 24 hours.

Formerly day and night were divided into four periods each, distinguished by beat of drum. The single beat, တချက်တီး tăh-jet-tee:, was at 9 o'clock in the morning; the double beat, နှစ်ချက်တီး hnăh-jet-tee:, at 12 noon; the သုံးချက်တီး thôhn:-jet-tee: at 3 p.m.; and လေးချက်တီး lay:-jet-tee: at 6 p.m.

Amongst the country people time was calculated in various ways, such as 'first cockcrow', ကြက်ဦးတွန် kyet-oo:-dŏŏn, about 2 a.m. ကြယ်နီပေါ် kyeh-nee-bāw, *when the red star rises* (morning); အာရုဏ်တက် āhyohn-det, *dawn*; သူငယ်အိပ်ဆိတ် thăh-gneh-ayk-sayt, *children's bedtime*; လူပျိုလှည့်ချိန် loo-byoh-hleh-jayn, *young man's courting time.* အာရုဏ် or more correctly အရုဏ် is the Pali အရုဏော Aruno, *Aurora the dawn.*

The expression ထမင်းအိုးတလုံးချက် htăhmin:-oh:-tăh-lohn:-jet, *the time it takes to boil a pot of rice,* is often used to denote a short time, and there are many others too numerous to mention.

Postal Rates.

The rates of postage between Burma and the United Kingdom are as follows, viz.—

From Burma to the United Kingdom: Letters, 1 anna (1*d.*) per ½ oz. Postcards, 1 anna, reply 2 annas; Printed papers, ½ anna per 50 grammes (½*d.* per 2 oz., about).

From the United Kingdom to Burma: Letters, 1*d.* per oz.; Postcards, 1*d.*; Printed papers, ½*d.* per 2 oz.